Lea   g   hKit
Programming

Addison-Wesley Learning Series

Visit **informit.com/learningseries** for a complete list of available publications.

The **Addison-Wesley Learning Series** is a collection of hands-on programming guides that help you quickly learn a new technology or language so you can apply what you've learned right away.

Each title comes with sample code for the application or applications built in the text. This code is fully annotated and can be reused in your own projects with no strings attached. Many chapters end with a series of exercises to encourage you to reexamine what you have just learned, and to tweak or adjust the code as a way of learning.

Titles in this series take a simple approach: they get you going right away and leave you with the ability to walk off and build your own application and apply the language or technology to whatever you are working on.

✦Addison-Wesley   **informIT** | Safari
the trusted technology learning source   Books Online

Learning WatchKit Programming

A Hands-On Guide to Creating
Apple Watch Applications

Wei-Meng Lee

✦✦Addison-Wesley

New York • Boston • Indianapolis • San Francisco
Toronto • Montreal • London • Munich • Paris • Madrid
Capetown • Sydney • Tokyo • Singapore • Mexico City

Library of Congress Control Number: 2015940909

Copyright © 2015 Pearson Education, Inc.

ISBN-13: 978-0-13-419544-5
ISBN-10: 0-13-419544-2

Text printed in the United States on recycled paper at RR Donnelley in Crawfordsville, Indiana.
First printing, June 2015

Editor-in-Chief
Mark L. Taub

Senior Acquisitions Editor
Trina MacDonald

Development Editor
Sheri Cain

Managing Editor
John Fuller

Full-Service Production Manager
Julie B. Nahil

Copy Editor
Stephanie Geels

Indexer
Jack Lewis

Proofreader
Anna Popick

Technical Reviewers
Mark H. Granoff
Chaim Krause
Niklas Saers

Editorial Assistant
Olivia Basegio

Cover Designer
Chuti Prasertsith

Compositor
CIP Group

❖

*I dedicate this book with love to my family, and to my dearest wife,
who has had to endure my irregular work schedule and take care
of things while I was trying to meet writing deadlines!*

❖

Contents at a Glance

Preface   **xiii**
Acknowledgments   **xvii**
About the Author   **xix**

1 Getting Started with WatchKit Programming   **1**

2 Apple Watch Interface Navigation   **17**

3 Apple Watch User Interface   **45**

4 Interfacing with iOS Apps   **99**

5 Displaying Notifications   **149**

6 Displaying Glances   **179**

Index   **195**

Contents

Preface   **xiii**

Acknowledgments   **xvii**

About the Author   **xix**

1 Getting Started with WatchKit Programming   1

Specifications of the Apple Watch   **1**

Getting the Tools for Development   **2**

Understanding the WatchKit App Architecture   **3**

Deploying Apple Watch Apps   **4**

Interaction between the Apple Watch and iPhone   **4**

Communicating with the Containing iOS App   **5**

Types of Apple Watch Applications   **6**

Hello, World!   **6**

Creating an iPhone Project   **6**

Adding a WatchKit App Target   **8**

Examining the Storyboard   **11**

WatchKit App Lifecycle   **12**

Modifying the Interface Controller   **13**

Running the Application on the Simulator   **14**

Summary   **16**

2 Apple Watch Interface Navigation   17

Interface Controllers and Storyboard   **17**

Lifecycle of an Interface Controller   **19**

Navigating between Interface Controllers   **22**

Hierarchical Navigation   **23**

Page-Based Navigation   **27**

Passing Data between Interface Controllers   **28**

Customizing the Title of the Chevron
or Cancel Button   **34**

Navigating Using Code   **35**

Presenting a Series of Pages   **38**

Changing the Current Page to Display   **40**

Summary   **43**

3   Apple Watch User Interface   45

Responding to User Interactions   45

    Button   46

    Switch   59

    Slider   62

Displaying Information   65

    Labels   65

    Images   65

    Table   71

Gathering Information   82

    Getting Text Inputs   82

    Getting Emojis   85

Laying Out the Controls   86

Force Touch   91

    Displaying a Context Menu   91

    Adding Menu Items Programmatically   97

Summary   98

4   Interfacing with iOS Apps   99

Localization   99

    Localizing the User Interface   102

    Creating Localizable Strings   106

    Using the Date Control   112

Communicating between the WatchKit App
and the Extension   113

    Location Data   114

    Displaying Maps   123

    Accessing Web Services   126

    Sharing Data   130

Summary   148

5   Displaying Notifications   149

What Is a Notification?   149

Types of Notifications on the Apple Watch   152

    Implementing the Short-Look Interface   153

    Implementing the Long-Look Interface   167

Summary   178

6 Displaying Glances   179

What Is a Glance?   **179**

    Implementing Glances   **180**

    Customizing the Glance   **182**

    Testing the Glance   **186**

Making the App Useful   **186**

    Creating a Shared App Group   **187**

    Implementing Background Fetch   **188**

Updating the Glance   **192**

Summary   **194**

Index   195

Preface

Welcome to *Learning WatchKit Programming*!

This is an exciting time to be a programmer, as we are witnessing a new era of wearables. While the Apple Watch is not the first wearable device in the market, its launch signified the intention of Apple to enter the wearable market in a big way. After successfully changing various industries—music, computer, phone, and mobile computing—Apple looks set to change the wearable industry. And nobody is taking this lightly.

As with the iPhone, much of the usefulness and functionality of the Apple Watch device actually come from the creativity of the third-party developers. In the early days of the iPhone, Apple restricted all third-party apps to web applications, as they wanted to retain the monopoly on developing natively for the device. However, due to the overwhelming protests of developers, Apple finally relented by releasing an SDK to support third-party apps. It was this decision that changed the fate of the iPhone; the iPhone would never have been so successful without the ability to support third-party apps.

When the Apple Watch was announced, Apple was quick to learn its lesson and realized that the success of the Apple Watch largely depends on the availability of apps that support it. Hence, before the release of the Apple Watch, the SDK was made available to developers to have a hand in developing Apple Watch apps.

The book you are holding in your hands right now (or reading on your phone or tablet) is a collection of tutorials that help you navigate the jungle of Apple Watch programming. This book contains all of the fundamental topics that you need to get started in Apple Watch programming. As this is a book on Apple Watch programming, I am going to make a couple of assumptions about you, the reader:

- You should already be familiar with the basics of developing an iOS application. In particular, concepts like outlets and actions should not be new to you.
- You should be comfortable with the Swift programming language. See the next section on how to get started with Swift if you are new to it.

What You'll Need

To get the most out of this book:

- You need a Mac, together with **Xcode**.
- Your Mac should be running at least **Mac OS X Yosemite (v10.10)**, or later.

- You can download the latest version of Xcode from the Mac App Store. All the code samples for this book are tested against Xcode 6.3.

- If you plan to test your apps on a real device, you need to register to become a paid iOS developer (https://developer.apple.com/programs/ios/). The program costs $99/year for individuals. Once registered, you can request a certificate to sign your apps so that they can be deployed onto your devices. To install your apps onto your devices, you also need to create provisioning profiles for your devices. Obviously, you also need an Apple Watch, which should be paired to your iPhone. The Apple Watch can only work with iPhone 5, iPhone 5c, iPhone 5s, iPhone 6, and iPhone 6 Plus.

- All code samples in this book can be tested and run on the iPhone Simulator without the need for a real device or Apple Watch. However, for some code examples, you need access to the iOS Developer Program and a valid provisioning profile in your applications before they can work. Hence, even if you do not have an Apple Watch and you do not intend to test the apps on a real device, you still need to have access to a paid iOS developer account to test some of the examples in this book.

- A number of examples in this book require an Internet connection in order to work, so ensure that you have an Internet connection when trying out the examples.

- All of the examples in this book are written in Swift. If you are not familiar with Swift, you can refer to my book *Beginning Swift Programming* (Wrox, 2014) for a jumpstart, or download my Swift Cheat Sheets at http://weimenglee.blogspot.sg/2014/11/swift-cheat-sheets-download-today.html.

How This Book Is Organized

This book is styled as a tutorial. You will be trying out the examples as I explain the concepts. This is a proven way to learn a new technology, and I strongly encourage you to type in the code as you work on the examples.

- **Chapter 1, Getting Started with WatchKit Programming**: In this chapter, you learn about the architecture of Apple Watch applications and how they tie in with your iOS apps. Most importantly, you get your chance to write a simple Apple Watch app and deploy it onto the simulator.

- **Chapter 2, Apple Watch Interface Navigation**: In this chapter, you dive deeper into how your Apple Watch application navigates between multiple screens. You get to see how data is passed between screens and how to customize the look and feel of each screen.

- **Chapter 3, Apple Watch User Interface**: Designing the user interface (UI) for your Apple Watch application is similar to designing for iPhone apps.

However, space is at a premium on the Apple Watch, and every millimeter on the screen must be put to good use in order to convey the exact intention of your app. In this chapter, you learn how to use the various UI controls in the Apple Watch to build your application.

- **Chapter 4, Interfacing with iOS Apps**: This chapter shows all the exciting features that you can add to your Apple Watch applications. You learn how to localize your apps, how to communicate between the watch app and the containing iOS app, how to call web services, and more!

- **Chapter 5, Displaying Notifications**: In this chapter, you learn how to display notifications on your Apple Watch. Notifications received by the iPhone are sent to the Apple Watch, and you have the chance to customize the notifications so that you can display the essence of the notifications quickly to the user.

- **Chapter 6, Displaying Glances**: Glances on the Apple Watch provide the user a quick way to gather information from apps. For example, Instagram's glance on the Apple Watch may show the most recently shared photo, while Twitter may show the latest trending tweets. In this chapter, you learn how to implement glances for your own apps.

About the Sample Code

The code samples in this book are written to provide the simplest way to understand core concepts without being bogged down with details like beautifying the UI or detailed error checking. The philosophy is to convey key ideas in the simplest manner possible. In real-life apps, you are expected to perform detailed error handling and to create a user-friendly UI for your apps. Although I do provide several scenarios in which a certain concept is useful, it is ultimately up to you, the reader, to exercise your creativity to put the concepts to work, and perhaps create the next killer app.

Getting the Sample Code

To download the sample code used in this book, visit the book's web page on Informit.com at informit.com/title/9780134195445 and click the **Extras** tab.

Contacting the Author

If you have any comments or questions about this book, please drop me an email at weimenglee@learn2develop.net, or stop by my web site at learn2develop.net.

Acknowledgments

Writing a book on emerging technology is always an exciting and perilous journey. On one end, you are dealing with the latest developments, going where not many have ventured, and on the other end you are dealing with many unknowns. To endure this journey you need a lot of help and family support. And I would like to take this opportunity to thank the people who make all this happen.

I am indebted to Trina MacDonald, senior acquisitions editor at Addison-Wesley/ Pearson Education, for giving me the chance to work on this book. She has always been supportive of my proposals for new titles, and I am really glad that we have the chance to work together on this project. Thank you very much for the opportunity and guidance, Trina! I hope I did not disappoint you.

I would like to thank the many heroes working behind the scene: copy editor Stephanie Geels, production editor Julie Nahil, and technical reviewers Mark H. Granoff, Chaim Krause, and Niklas Saers for turning the manuscript into a book that I am proud of!

Last but not least, I want to thank my family for all the support that they have always given me. Without their encouragement, this book would never have been possible.

About the Author

Wei-Meng Lee is a technologist and founder of Developer Learning Solutions (learn2develop.net), a technology company specializing in hands-on training on the latest web and mobile technologies. Wei-Meng speaks regularly at international conferences and has authored and coauthored numerous books on .NET, XML, Android, and iOS technologies. He writes extensively for informIT.com and mobiForge.com.

Getting Started with WatchKit Programming

*Design is a funny word. Some people think design means how it
looks. But of course, if you dig deeper, it's really how it works.*

Steve Jobs

Apple Watch is a smartwatch created by Apple and officially announced by Tim Cook during the September 9, 2014, Apple event. It is touted as the next big thing after the launch of the iPhone and the iPad, and is expected to change the rules of wearables (just as the iPhone changed the smartphone industry and the iPad changed the tablet industry).

In this chapter, you learn about the architecture of Apple Watch applications and how they tie in with your iOS apps. Most importantly, you get your hands dirty by writing a simple Apple Watch app and deploying it onto the simulator.

Specifications of the Apple Watch

The Apple Watch is powered using a custom chip (dubbed the S1) from Apple. The back of the Apple Watch is a heart rate sensor, which is a set of LEDs and photodiodes mounted in a ceramic cover. The watch also has an accelerometer, WiFi, Bluetooth Low Energy (LE), and GPS. It is charged wirelessly using a magnetic charger (much like the MagSafe chargers that come with the MacBook and MacBook Pro), which snaps to the back of the watch.

The Apple Watch comes in two sizes (see Figure 1.1):

- **38mm watch (small)**: Resolution of 272 pixels by 340 pixels
- **42mm watch (large)**: Resolution of 312 pixels by 390 pixels

Figure 1.1   The resolutions of the Apple Watch sizes

To interact with the Apple Watch, you can use the following:

- **Digital Crown**: Allows you to scroll through lists of items, as well as zoom in or out of images, etc. The Digital Crown also acts as a Home button—pressing it returns you to the Home screen.
- **Force Touch**: A pressure-sensitive touchscreen, allowing it to tell the difference between a tap and a press.
- **Taptic Engine**: A haptic feedback system, which taps on your wrist to inform you of notifications and vibrates when you rotate the Digital Crown.

Getting the Tools for Development

To develop Apple Watch applications, you need Xcode 6.3 or later, which you can download from the Mac App Store.

Xcode 6.3

This examples in this book were written and tested using Xcode 6.3. At the time of writing, Xcode 6.4 is in beta. Hence, you should expect to see some minor changes in screenshots in this book when the final release of Xcode 6.4 is available.

Xcode 6.3 contains the WatchKit, the framework that is used to create Apple Watch applications. In addition, Xcode 6.3 also comes with the Apple Watch Simulator, which allows you to test your Apple Watch application without using a real device.

What Is WatchKit?

WatchKit is a framework (similar to other frameworks such as the CoreLocation or MapKit, for those of you familiar with iOS development) that contains all the classes that are necessary to create Apple Watch applications.

Understanding the WatchKit App Architecture

To run third-party apps, Apple Watch requires the presence of an iPhone. An Apple Watch application consists of two components (technically known as *bundles*):

- A *WatchKit app* that runs on the Apple Watch
- A *WatchKit Extension* that runs on the iPhone

Note

The Apple Watch is compatible with iPhone 5, iPhone 5c, iPhone 5s, iPhone 6, and iPhone 6 Plus running iOS 8.3 or later.

Figure 1.2 shows the relationship between the two bundles. The two bundles communicate with each other using a Bluetooth LE connection. The WatchKit framework encapsulates all the communication details, and it is totally transparent to the developer.

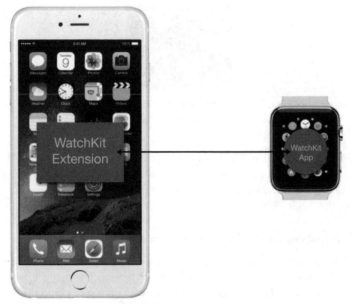

Figure 1.2   The relationship between two bundles that make up
an Apple Watch application

The WatchKit app only contains the storyboards and resources needed to create the user interface of your Apple Watch application; the code for managing the interactions with your Apple Watch application resides in the WatchKit Extension.

> **Note**
>
> The WatchKit app does not contain any source code files. All source code is to be executed in the WatchKit Extension running on the iPhone.

Deploying Apple Watch Apps

Because of the tight integration between the WatchKit app and WatchKit Extension, the two bundles are packaged together within a single iOS app bundle (see Figure 1.3). So, to develop an Apple Watch application, you first need to develop an iPhone application.

Figure 1.3   The WatchKit Extension and the WatchKit app
must be bundled within an iOS app bundle

When the user installs an iOS application containing the WatchKit and WatchKit Extension, he would be prompted to install the WatchKit app if a paired Apple Watch is available. Once the WatchKit app is installed on the Apple Watch, it can be launched directly from the Apple Watch home screen.

Interaction between the Apple Watch and iPhone

Figure 1.4 shows how the WatchKit app (running on the Apple Watch) interacts with the WatchKit Extension (running on the iPhone). Whenever the user interacts with the WatchKit app, all interactions are handled by the WatchKit Extension through the WatchKit framework. The WatchKit framework uses Bluetooth LE to communicate between the Apple Watch and iPhone. As an Apple Watch developer, you don't have to worry about what goes on behind the scenes.

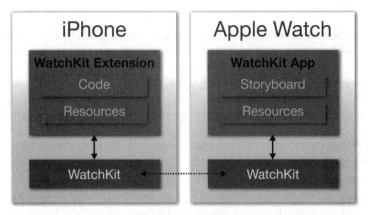

Figure 1.4   Interactions with the WatchKit app are handled by the WatchKit Extension through the WatchKit framework

Communicating with the Containing iOS App

The WatchKit Extension runs only when the WatchKit app is running and it does not support background execution. Hence, for tasks that might take a bit of time to complete (such as getting location data or consuming web services), it is advisable to send the request to the containing iOS to perform the tasks, which can be configured to run in the background (see Figure 1.5).

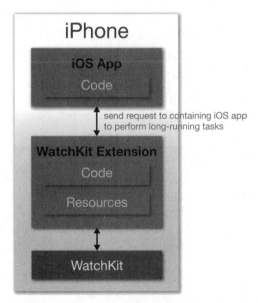

Figure 1.5   Long-performing tasks should be delegated to the containing iOS app to perform in the background

> **Note**
>
> Chapter 2, "Apple Watch Interface Navigation," demonstrates how to send requests from the WatchKit Extension to the containing iOS app to perform long-running tasks.

Types of Apple Watch Applications

For this release of WatchKit, you can develop three types of Apple Watch applications:

- **WatchKit Apps**: Apps that run on the Apple Watch and interact with the application logic running on the iPhone.
- **Glances**: A supplemental way for the user to view important information from your app. Glances does not support interactions with users—tapping on a glance launches the WatchKit app. Chapter 6, "Displaying Glances," discusses glances in more details.
- **Notifications**: Displays notifications received by the iPhone (either local or remote notifications); apps can customize the notification interface. (Chapter 5, "Displaying Notifications," discusses notifications.)

Hello, World!

Now that we have all the basics covered, you must be raring to go and yearning to get your hands dirty! So, without further ado, make sure you download and install Xcode and let's create your first Apple Watch app!

Creating an iPhone Project

The first step toward creating an Apple Watch application is to create an iPhone application. To do this, follow these steps:

1. Launch Xcode and select the **Single View Application** template (see Figure 1.6).
2. Click **Next**.
3. Name the project as follows (see Figure 1.7):

   Product Name: HelloAppleWatch

   Organization Name: Either your name or your organization's name

   Organization Identifier: Usually the reverse domain name of your organization (e.g., *com.example*). The Bundle Identifier is formed by concatenating the Organization Name with the Product Name. If you intend to host your app on the App Store, the Bundle Identifier of your app must be unique.

   Language: Swift

   Devices: iPhone

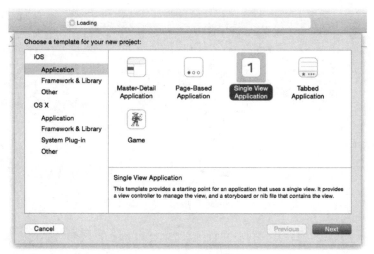

Figure 1.6   Creating a Single View Application project in Xcode

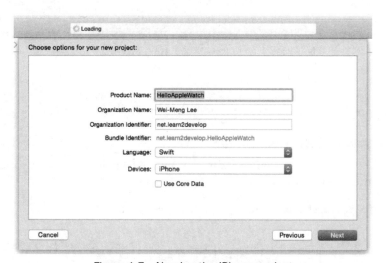

Figure 1.7   Naming the iPhone project

4. Click **Next**.
5. Select a folder on your Mac to save the project, and click **Create**.

   When the project is created successfully, you will see Xcode, as shown in Figure 1.8.

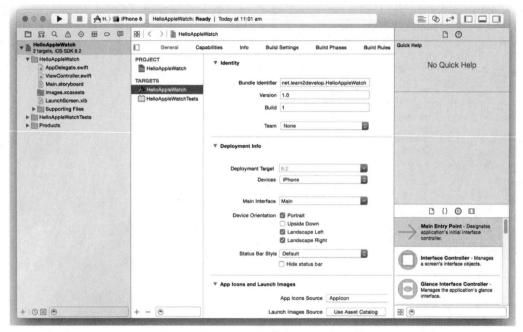

Figure 1.8   The project created in Xcode

So far, this process describes the creation of an iPhone application. In the next section, you learn how to add the WatchKit Extension and the WatchKit app to the project.

Adding a WatchKit App Target

To add the WatchKit Extension and WatchKit app to the project, you need to add a target to it. Here's how to do this:

1. In Xcode, select **File | New | Target...** (see Figure 1.9).

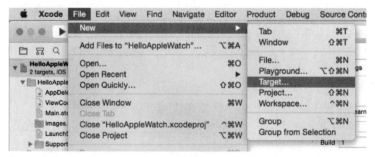

Figure 1.9   To develop an Apple Watch application, you need to add a
Target to your iPhone project

2. Under the iOS section on the left (see Figure 1.10), select **Apple Watch** and then select the **WatchKit App** template on the right. Click **Next**.

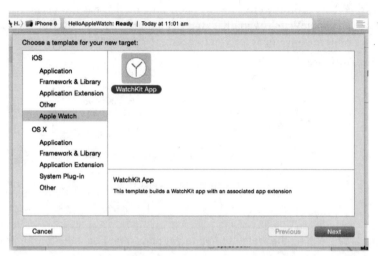

Figure 1.10   Select the WatchKit App target to add to the current project

3. You are prompted with a dialog that's shown in Figure 1.11. For the most part, you don't have to change anything. Just uncheck the option Include Notification Scene so that we can keep the WatchKit project to a bare minimum. Click **Finish**.

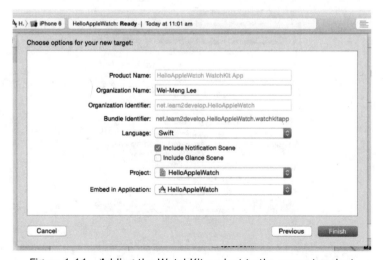

Figure 1.11   Adding the WatchKit project to the current project

> **Note**
>
> Chapter 5 discusses notifications and Chapter 6 discusses glances in more detail.

Next, you are prompted to activate a new scheme that has just been created for you: HelloAppleWatch WatchKit App (see Figure 1.12). Activating this scheme makes it more convenient for you to debug the Apple Watch application.

4. Click **Activate**.

Figure 1.12   Adding the WatchKit App target adds a new scheme to your project

The project should now look like Figure 1.13.

Figure 1.13   The three main components of the project: the containing iOS app, the WatchKit Extension, and the WatchKit app

In particular, observe the three highlighted groups:

- **HelloAppleWatch**: The iOS app that acts as the container for the WatchKit app
- **HelloAppleWatch WatchKit Extension**: The WatchKit Extension that runs on the iPhone
- **HelloAppleWatch WatchKit App**: The WatchKit app that runs on the Apple Watch

Observe that the HelloAppleWatch WatchKit App group contains the Interface .storyboard file. This is the storyboard file that contains the UI of your Apple Watch app. The HelloAppleWatch WatchKit Extension group, on the other hand, contains the InterfaceController.swift file, which is the code that is executed when the user interacts with the Apple Watch app.

Examining the Storyboard

Let's look at the Interface.storyboard file located in the HelloAppleWatch WatchKit App group. Selecting the file displays it using the Storyboard Editor (see Figure 1.14). It contains a single Interface Controller, which is similar to a View Controller in your

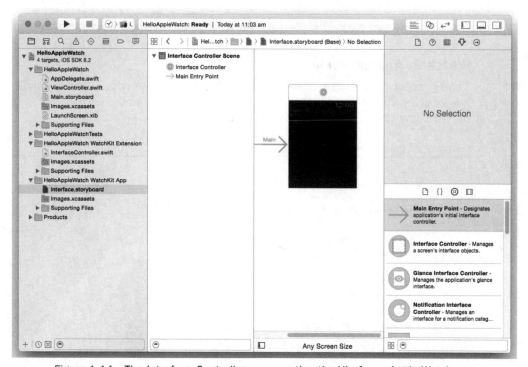

Figure 1.14   The Interface Controller representing the UI of your Apple Watch app

iPhone application. When the user loads the application on his Apple Watch, the initial Interface Controller from the main storyboard is loaded.

When you select the Interface Controller and examine the Class attribute under the Identity Inspector window, you will see that it is connected to a class known as `InterfaceController` (see Figure 1.15).

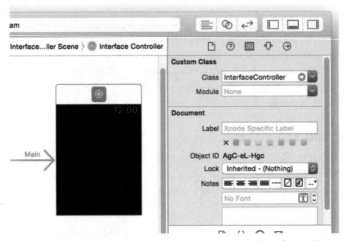

Figure 1.15   The class representing the Interface Controller

WatchKit App Lifecycle

The `InterfaceController` class is stored in the file named InterfaceController.swift. It is located within the HelloAppleWatch WatchKit Extension group. Listing 1.1 shows the content of the `InterfaceController` class.

Listing 1.1   **Content of the `InterfaceController` Class**

```
import WatchKit
import Foundation

class InterfaceController: WKInterfaceController {

    override func awakeWithContext(context: AnyObject?) {
        super.awakeWithContext(context)

        // Configure interface objects here.
    }

    override func willActivate() {
        // This method is called when watch view controller is about to
        // be visible to user
        super.willActivate()
    }
```

```
override func didDeactivate() {
    // This method is called when watch view controller is no longer
    // visible
    super.didDeactivate()
}
```

}

The `InterfaceController` class is a subclass of the `WKInterfaceController` class. When subclassing the `WKInterfaceController` class, you can override a couple of methods to handle the lifecycle of an Interface Controller:

- **init**—The designated initializer for the Interface Controller objects. Note that Xcode does not create this method by default.
- **awakeWithContext:**—Fired when the Interface Controller is displayed for the first time; useful for object initializations, updating your UI, etc.
- **willActivate**—Fired when the user interface is visible to the user; useful for updating the user interface, setting up timers, etc.
- **didDeactivate**—Fired when the user exits your app explicitly or stops interacting with the Apple Watch; useful for cleaning up resources, saving data, etc.

Note
Chapter 2 discusses the lifecycles of the Interface View Controller in more detail.

Modifying the Interface Controller

Now that we have discussed the underlying details of the parts that make everything work, it is time to do something visual and fun! In the Interface Controller found inside the Interface.storyboard file, drag and drop a Label view (from the Object Library) onto it (see Figure 1.16).

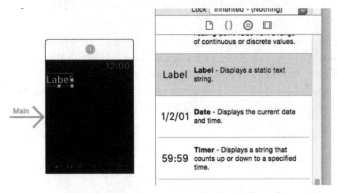

Figure 1.16   Adding a Label view to the Interface Controller

Double-click the Label view and type **Hello, World!**, as shown in Figure 1.17.

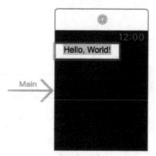

Figure 1.17   Typing some text into the Label view

Running the Application on the Simulator

Finally, you are ready to test the application on the iPhone Simulator. In Xcode, you need to first set the scheme to HelloAppleWatch WatckKit App (see Figure 1.18). Also, ensure that the iPhone 6 Simulator is selected. Once this is done, press Command-R to deploy the application onto the iPhone Simulator.

Figure 1.18   Ensure that the HelloAppleWatch WatchKit App
scheme is selected before running the project

When the iPhone Simulator is launched, your iPhone app will be installed on the iPhone 6 Simulator, but it will not be launched. This is because the scheme selected was HelloAppleWatch WatckKit App, and hence only the WatchKit app will run. If you do not see the Apple Watch Simulator, you can go to **Hardware | External Displays** and select one of the watch's sizes (see Figure 1.19).

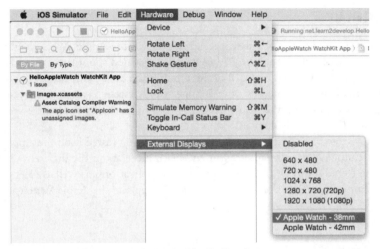

Figure 1.19   Selecting the Apple Watch Simulator you want to display

You should now see the Apple Watch Simulator running the application (see Figure 1.20).

Figure 1.20   Your first Apple Watch application
running on the Apple Watch Simulator

Summary

In this chapter, you learned the basics of developing for the Apple Watch. You first read about the specifications of the watch, and then you learned about the architecture of third-party apps that you can build. Most importantly, the bulk of the processing of your Apple Watch app is performed on your iPhone. This strategy is important because reducing the workload on the watch drastically improves the battery life of your watch, a crucial issue for wearable devices.

You also wrote your first Apple Watch application and tested it on the Apple Watch Simulator. In the next few chapters, you will learn more about the different views that you can use to build the UI of your Apple Watch applications, as well as topics such as how to communicate between the containing iOS app and the Apple Watch app.

2

Apple Watch Interface Navigation

It's really hard to design products by focus groups. A lot of times, people don't know what they want until you show it to them.

Steve Jobs

In Chapter 1, "Getting Started with WatchKit Programming," you learned about the various specifications and features of the Apple Watch. You also had the chance to use Xcode to create a simple iPhone project that supports the Apple Watch. You then used the Apple Watch Simulator to test the application. In this chapter, you dive into how your Apple Watch application navigates between multiple screens.

Interface Controllers and Storyboard

As you learned in Chapter 1, the user interface of your Apple Watch application is encapsulated in a storyboard file. Within the storyboard file, you have an Interface Controller that represents a screen on the Apple Watch. In this section, let's create a project so that we can examine the storyboard in more detail:

1. Using Xcode, create a Single View Application project and name it **LifeCycle**.

2. Add the WatchKit App target to the project. Uncheck the option Include Notification Scene so that we can keep the WatchKit project to a bare minimum.

   > **Note**
   >
   > If you are not sure how to add the WatchKit App target to the existing project, refer to Chapter 1.

3. Once the target is added to the project, select the Interface.storyboard file located within the LifeCycle WatchKit App group (see Figure 2.1). This opens the file using the Storyboard Editor.

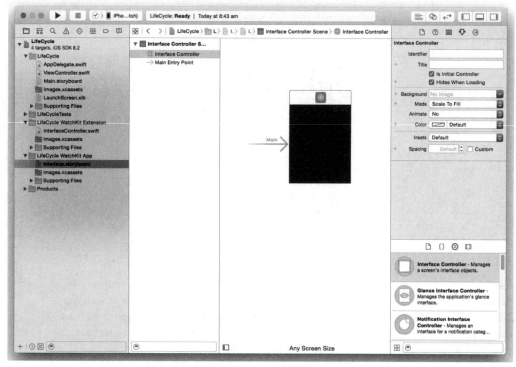

Figure 2.1   Editing the storyboard file

4. Select the Interface Controller and view its Identity Inspector window (see Figure 2.2). The Class is set to InterfaceController, which means that it is represented by a Swift class named InterfaceController.

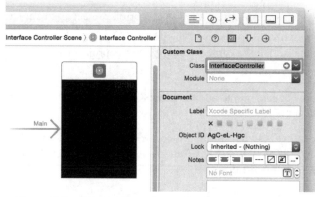

Figure 2.2   The Interface Controller is represented by a Swift class named InterfaceController

5. View its Attributes Inspector window and observe that the Is Initial Controller attribute is checked (see Figure 2.3). This attribute indicates that, when the application is loaded, this is the default Interface Controller that will be displayed.

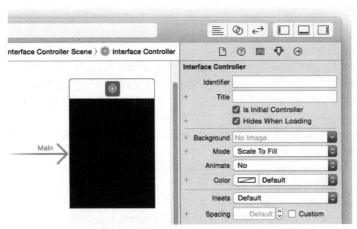

Figure 2.3   The Is Initial Controller attribute indicates that the current Interface Controller will be displayed when the application loads

Lifecycle of an Interface Controller

As you have seen in the previous section and in Chapter 1, an Interface Controller is connected to a Swift class located in the WatchKit Extension group of the project. In this example, this Swift class is named InterfaceController.swift. It has the following content:

```
import WatchKit
import Foundation

class InterfaceController: WKInterfaceController {

    override func awakeWithContext(context: AnyObject?) {
        super.awakeWithContext(context)

        // Configure interface objects here.
    }

    override func willActivate() {
        // This method is called when watch view controller is about to
        // be visible to user
        super.willActivate()
    }
```

```
override func didDeactivate() {
    // This method is called when watch view controller is no longer visible
    super.didDeactivate()
}
}
```

Specifically, it has three key methods:

- **awakeWithContext:**—The system calls this method at initialization time, passing it any contextual data from a previous Interface Controller. You should use this method to initialize and to prepare your UI for display, as well as to obtain any data that is passed to it from another Interface Controller (you will learn how this is done in the later section on passing data).

- **willActivate**—This method is called by the system when the Interface Controller is about to be displayed. You should use this method to make some last-minute changes to your UI and to refrain from performing any tasks that initialize the UI—these should be done in the awakeWithContext method.

- **didDeactivate**—This method is called when the Interface Controller is no longer onscreen. You should use this method to perform cleanup operations on your Interface Controller, such as invalidating timers or saving state-related information.

Besides the three methods just discussed, you can also add an initializer to the Interface Controller class:

```
override init() {
    super.init()
}
```

You can also perform initialization for your Interface Controller in this initializer, but you should leave the bulk of the UI initialization to the awakeWithContext method.

Let's try an example to better understand the use of the various methods:

1. Add the following statements in bold to the InterfaceController.swift file:

```
import WatchKit
import Foundation

class InterfaceController: WKInterfaceController {

    override init() {
        super.init()
        println("In the init initializer")
    }

    override func awakeWithContext(context: AnyObject?) {
        super.awakeWithContext(context)
```

```swift
        // Configure interface objects here.
        println("In the awakeWithContext event")
    }

    override func willActivate() {
        // This method is called when watch view controller is about to be
        // visible to user
        super.willActivate()
        println("In the willActivate event")
    }

    override func didDeactivate() {
        // This method is called when watch view controller is no longer
        // visible
        super.didDeactivate()
        println("In the didDeactivate event")
    }

}
```

2. Run the application on the iPhone 6 Simulator. When the application is loaded onto the Apple Watch Simulator, you should see the statements printed out in the Output Window in Xcode, as shown in Figure 2.4. Observe that the `init`, `awakeWithContext:`, and `willActivate` methods are fired when the Interface Controller is loaded.

> **Note**
>
> If you are not able to see the Output Window, press Command-Shift-C in Xcode.

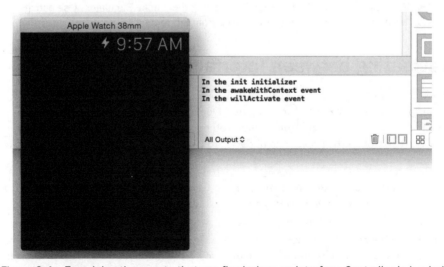

Figure 2.4   Examining the events that are fired when an Interface Controller is loaded

3. With the Apple Watch Simulator selected, select **Hardware | Lock** to lock
   the Apple Watch. Observe the output in the Output window (see Figure 2.5).
   Observe that the `didDeactivate` method is now executed.

> **Note**
>
> The `didDeactivate` method will also be fired when an Interface Controller tran-
> sits to another Interface Controller.

Figure 2.5   Examining the event that is fired when an Interface Controller is deactivated

> **Note**
>
> To unlock the Apple Watch Simulator, unlock the iPhone Simulator by selecting
> **Hardware | Home**, and then by swiping from left to right.

Navigating between Interface Controllers

The basic unit of display for an Apple Watch app is represented by an Interface Controller (of type `WKInterfaceController`). Depending on the type of application
you are working on, there are times where you need to spread your UI across multiple
Interface Controllers. In Apple Watch, there are two ways to navigate between Interface
Controllers:

- **Hierarchical**: Pushes another Interface Controller on the screen. This model is
  usually used when you want the user to follow a series of related steps in order to
  perform a particular action.

- **Page-based**: Displays another Interface Controller on top of the current Interface Controller. This model is usually used if the information displayed on each

Interface Controller is not closely related to other Interface Controller. You can also use this model to display a series of Interface Controllers, which the user can select by swiping the screen.

Similarities to iPhone Development

The page-based navigation method is similar to presenting a modal View Controller in iPhone, whereas the hierarchical navigation method is similar to using a navigation controller in iPhone.

Hierarchical Navigation

A hierarchical interface always starts with a root Interface Controller. It then pushes additional Interface Controllers when a button or a control in a screen is tapped.

1. Using Xcode, create a Single View Application project and name it UINavigation.
2. Add a WatchKit App target to the project. Uncheck the option Include Notification Scene so that we can keep the WatchKit project to a bare minimum.
3. In the UINavigation WatchKit App group, select the Interface.storyboard file to edit it in the Storyboard Editor.
4. Drag and drop another Interface Controller object onto the editor, as shown in Figure 2.6. You should now have two Interface Controllers.

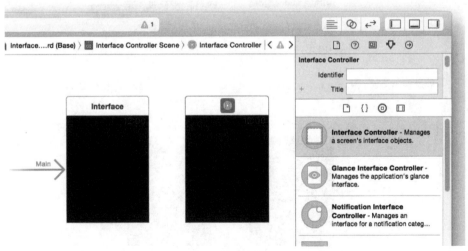

Figure 2.6   Adding another Interface Controller to the storyboard

5. In the original Interface Controller, add a Button control (see Figure 2.7) and change its title (by double-clicking it) to **Next Screen**.

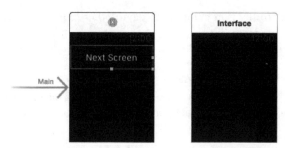

Figure 2.7   Adding a Button control to the first Interface Controller

6. Control-click the **Next Screen** button and drag and drop it over the second
   Interface Controller (see Figure 2.8).

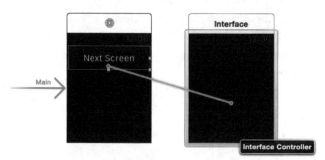

Figure 2.8   Control-click the Button control and drag
and drop it over the second Interface Controller

7. You will see a popup called Action Segue. Select **push** (see Figure 2.9).

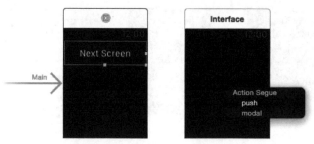

Figure 2.9   Creating a push segue

8. A segue will now be created (see Figure 2.10), linking the first Interface Controller to the second.

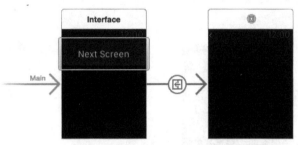

Figure 2.10   The segue that is created after performing the action

9. Select the segue and set its Identifier to **hierarchical** in the Attributes Inspector window (see Figure 2.11). This identifier allows us to identify it programmatically in our code later.

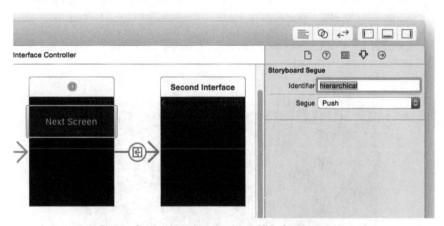

Figure 2.11   Naming the Identifier for the segue

10. Add a Label control to the second Interface Controller, as shown in Figure 2.12. Set the Lines attribute of the Label control to **0** in the Attributes Inspector window so that the Label can wrap around long text (used later in this chapter).

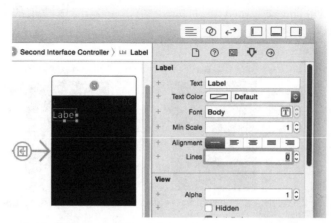

Figure 2.12   Adding a Label control to the second Interface Controller

11. You are now ready to test the application. Run the application on the iPhone 6 Simulator and, in the Apple Watch Simulator, click the **Next Screen** button and observe that the application navigates to the second Interface Controller containing the Label control (see Figure 2.13). Also, observe that the second Interface Controller has a < icon (known as a *chevron*) displayed in the top-left corner. Clicking it returns the application to the first Interface Controller.

Figure 2.13   Navigating to another Interface Controller using hierarchical navigation

Note

At this point, the Label control on the second Interface Controller is still displaying the default text "Label." In later sections in this chapter, you learn how to pass data from the first Interface Controller to the second and then how to display the data in the Label control.

Page-Based Navigation

You can also display an Interface Controller modally. This is useful if you want to obtain some information from the user or get the user to confirm an action.

1. Using the same project created in the previous section, add another Button control to the first Interface Controller, as shown in Figure 2.14. Change the title of the Button to **Display Screen**.

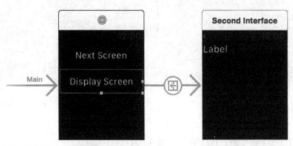

Figure 2.14   Adding another Button control to the first Interface Controller

2. Create a segue connecting the Display Screen button to the second Interface Controller. In the Action Segue popup that appears, select **modal**. Set the Identifier of the newly created segue to **pagebased** (see Figure 2.15).

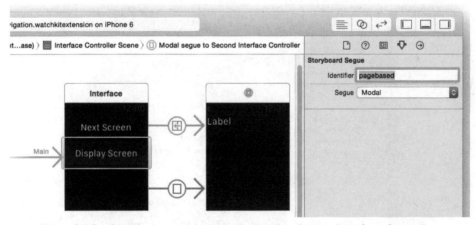

Figure 2.15   Creating a modal segue connecting the two Interface Controllers

3. Run the application on the iPhone 6 Simulator and, in the Apple Watch Simulator, click the **Display Screen** button and observe that the second Interface Controller appears from the bottom of the screen. Also, observe that the second Interface Controller now has a Cancel button displayed in the top-left corner (see Figure 2.16). Clicking it hides the second Interface Controller.

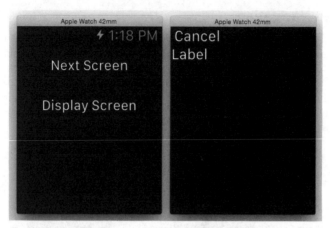

Figure 2.16   Displaying another Interface Controller modally

Passing Data between Interface Controllers

In the previous sections, you saw how to make your Apple Watch application transit from one Interface Controller to another, using either the hierarchical or page-based navigation method. One commonly performed task is to pass data from one Interface Controller to another. In this section, you do just that.

1. Using the UINavigation project that you used in the previous section, right-click the **UINavigation WatchKit Extension** group and select **New File...** (see Figure 2.17).

Figure 2.17   Adding a new file to the project

2. Select the **Cocoa Touch Class** (see Figure 2.18) template and click **Next**.

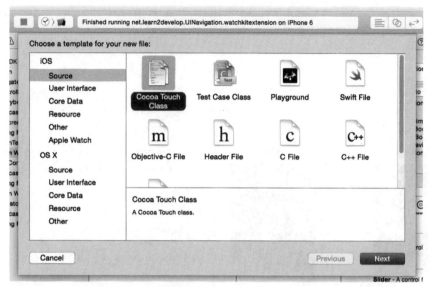

Figure 2.18   Selecting the Cocoa Touch Class template

3. Name the Class SecondInterfaceController and make it a subclass of WKInterfaceController (see Figure 2.19). Click **Next**.

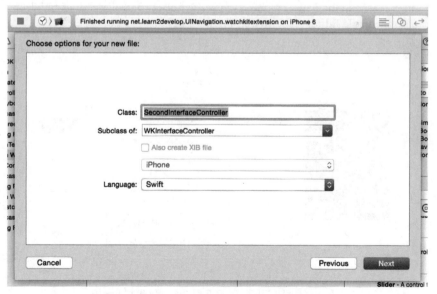

Figure 2.19   Naming the newly added class

4. A file named SecondInterfaceController.swift will now be added to the UINavigation WatchKit Extension group of your project.

5. Back in the Storyboard Editor, select the second Interface Controller and set its Class (in the Identity Inspector window) to `SecondInterfaceController` (see Figure 2.20).

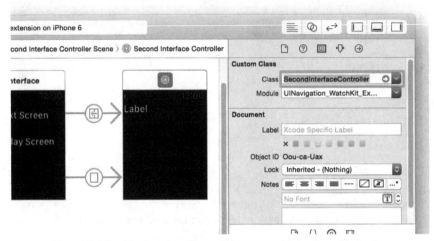

Figure 2.20   Setting the class of the second Interface Controller

6. Select the **View | Assistant Editor | Show Assistant Editor** menu item to show the Assistant Editor. Control-click the **Label** control and drag and drop it onto the Code Editor (as shown in Figure 2.21).

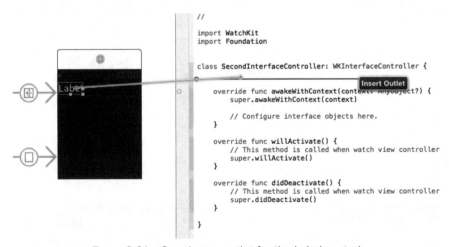

Figure 2.21   Creating an outlet for the Label control

7. Create an outlet and name it `label` (see Figure 2.22).

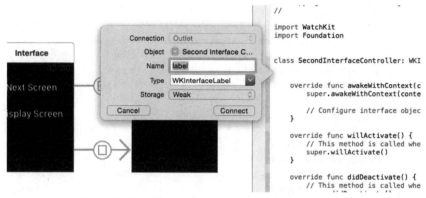

Figure 2.22   Naming the outlet for the Label control

8. An outlet is now added to the code:

```
import WatchKit
import Foundation

class SecondInterfaceController: WKInterfaceController {

    @IBOutlet weak var label: WKInterfaceLabel!

    override func awakeWithContext(context: AnyObject?) {
        super.awakeWithContext(context)

        // Configure interface objects here.
    }

    override func willActivate() {
        // This method is called when watch view controller is about to be
        // visible to user
        super.willActivate()
    }

    override func didDeactivate() {
        // This method is called when watch view controller is no longer
        // visible
        super.didDeactivate()
    }
}
```

9. Add the following statements in bold to the InterfaceController.swift file:

```
import WatchKit
import Foundation


class InterfaceController: WKInterfaceController {

    override func awakeWithContext(context: AnyObject?) {
        super.awakeWithContext(context)

        // Configure interface objects here.
    }

    override func willActivate() {
        // This method is called when watch view controller is about to be
        // visible to user
        super.willActivate()
    }

    override func didDeactivate() {
        // This method is called when watch view controller is no longer
        // visible
        super.didDeactivate()
    }

    override func contextForSegueWithIdentifier(segueIdentifier: String) ->
        AnyObject? {
            if segueIdentifier == "hierarchical" {
                return ["segue": "hierarchical",
                    "data":"Passed through hierarchical navigation"]
            } else if segueIdentifier == "pagebased" {
                return ["segue": "pagebased",
                    "data": "Passed through page-based navigation"]
            } else {
                return ["segue": "", "data": ""]
            }
    }

}
```

The contextForSegueWithIdentifier: method is fired before any of the
segues fire (when the user taps on one of the Button controls). Here, you check
the identifier of the segue (through the segueIdentifier argument). Specifically, you return a dictionary containing two keys: segue and data.

10. Add the following statements in bold to the SecondInterfaceController.swift file:

```
import WatchKit
import Foundation
```

```
class SecondInterfaceController: WKInterfaceController {

    @IBOutlet weak var label: WKInterfaceLabel!

    override func awakeWithContext(context: AnyObject?) {
        super.awakeWithContext(context)

        // Configure interface objects here.
        var dict = context as? NSDictionary
        if dict != nil {
            var segue = dict!["segue"] as! String
            var data = dict!["data"] as! String
            self.label.setText(data)
        }
    }
}
```

When the second Interface Controller is loaded, you retrieve the data that is passed into it in the awakeWithContext: method through the context argument. Since the first Interface Controller passes in a dictionary, you can typecast it into an NSDictionary object and then retrieve the value of the segue and data keys. The value of the data key is then displayed in the Label control.

11. Run the application on the iPhone 6 Simulator and in the Apple Watch Simulator, click the **Next Screen** button, and observe the string displayed in the second Interface Controller (see Figure 2.23).

Figure 2.23   Displaying the data passed through the hierarchical navigation

12. Click the **<** chevron to return to the first Interface Controller and click the **Display Screen** button. Observe the string displayed in the second Interface Controller (see Figure 2.24).

Figure 2.24   Displaying the data passed through the page-based navigation

Customizing the Title of the Chevron or Cancel Button

As you have seen in the previous section, a chevron is displayed when you push an Interface Controller using the hierarchical navigation method. A default Cancel button is displayed when you display an Interface Controller modally. However, the chevron or Cancel button can be customized.

1. Add the following statements in bold to the SecondInterfaceController.swift file:

```
import WatchKit
import Foundation

class SecondInterfaceController: WKInterfaceController {

    @IBOutlet weak var label: WKInterfaceLabel!

    override func awakeWithContext(context: AnyObject?) {
        super.awakeWithContext(context)

        // Configure interface objects here.
        var dict = context as? NSDictionary
        if dict != nil {
            var segue = dict!["segue"] as! String
            var data = dict!["data"] as! String
            self.label.setText(data)
            if segue == "pagebased" {
                self.setTitle("Close")
            } else {
                self.setTitle("Back")
            }
        }
    }
```

2. Run the application on the iPhone 6 Simulator and in the Apple Watch Simulator, click the **Next Screen** button, and observe the string displayed next to the chevron (see Figure 2.25).

Figure 2.25   Displaying a string next to the chevron

3. Click the **<Back** chevron to return to the first Interface Controller and click the **Display Screen** button. Observe that the Cancel button is now displayed as Close (see Figure 2.26).

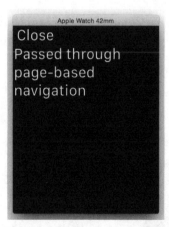

Figure 2.26   Modifying the button for a modal Interface Controller

Navigating Using Code

Although you can link up Interface Controllers by creating segues in your storyboard, it is not versatile. In a real-life application, the flow of your application may depend on certain conditions being met, and hence, you need to be able to decide during runtime which Interface Controller to navigate to (or display modally).

1. Using Xcode, create a new Single View Application project and name it **NavigateUsingCode**.

2. Add a WatchKit App target to the project. Uncheck the option Include Notification Scene so that we can keep the WatchKit project to a bare minimum.

3. Click the **Interface.storyboard** file located in the NavigateUsingCode WatchKit App group in your project to edit it using the Storyboard Editor.

4. Add two Button controls to the first Interface Controller and then add another Interface Controller to the storyboard. In the second Interface Controller, add a Label control, as shown in Figure 2.27.

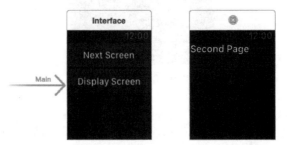

Figure 2.27   Populating the two Interface Controllers

5. Select the second Interface Controller and set its Identifier attribute (in the Attributes Inspector window) to **secondpage**, as shown in Figure 2.28.

Figure 2.28   Setting the Identifier for the second Interface Controller

6. In the first Interface Controller, create two actions (one for each button) and name them as shown here in the InterfaceController.swift file. You should create the actions by control-dragging them from the storyboard onto the Code Editor:

```swift
import WatchKit
import Foundation

class InterfaceController: WKInterfaceController {

    @IBAction func btnNextScreen() {
    }

    @IBAction func btnDisplayScreen() {
    }
```

7. Add the following statements to the two actions in the InterfaceController.swift file:

```swift
import WatchKit
import Foundation

class InterfaceController: WKInterfaceController {

    @IBAction func btnNextScreen() {
        pushControllerWithName("secondpage", context: nil)
    }

    @IBAction func btnDisplayScreen() {
        presentControllerWithName("secondpage", context: nil)
    }
```

Observe that the first button uses the pushControllerWithName:context: method to perform a hierarchical navigation. The first argument to this method takes in the identifier of the Interface Controller to navigate to (which we had earlier set in Step 5). The context argument allows you to pass data to the target Interface Controller, which in this case we simply set to nil. For the second button, we use the presentControllerWithName:context: method to perform a page-based navigation. Like the pushControllerWithName:context: method, the first argument is the identifier of the Interface Controller to display, whereas the second argument allows you to pass data to the target Interface Controller.

8. Run the application on the iPhone 6 Simulator. Clicking either button brings you to the second Interface Controller (see Figure 2.29).

Figure 2.29   Navigating the Interface Controllers programmatically

Returning to the Previous Screen

Although you can return to the previous screen by tapping either the chevron or the **Cancel** button, you can also programmatically return to the previous screen. If you navigate to an Interface Controller using the `pushControllerWithName:context:` method, you can programmatically return to the Interface Controller using the corresponding `popController` method. If you display an Interface Controller using the `presentControllerWithName:context:` method, you can dismiss the current Interface Controller using the corresponding `dismissController` method.

Presenting a Series of Pages

For page-based applications, you can display more than one single Interface Controller modally—you can display a series of them.

1. Using the same project created in the previous section, add a third Interface Controller to the storyboard and add a Label control to it. Set the Label text to **Third Page** (see Figure 2.30).

2. Set the Identifier attribute of the third Interface Controller to **thirdpage** in the Attributes Inspector window (see Figure 2.31).

3. Add the following statements in bold to the InterfaceController.swift file:

```
@IBAction func btnDisplayScreen() {
    //presentControllerWithName("secondpage", context: nil)
    presentControllerWithNames(["secondpage", "thirdpage"], contexts: nil)
}
```

Instead of using the `presentControllerWithName:context:` method, we now use the `presentControllerWithNames:context:` method. The only difference between the two methods is that the latter takes in an array of string in the first argument. This array of string contains the identifiers of Interface Controllers that you want to display.

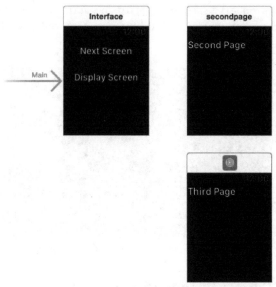

Figure 2.30   Adding the third Interface Controller

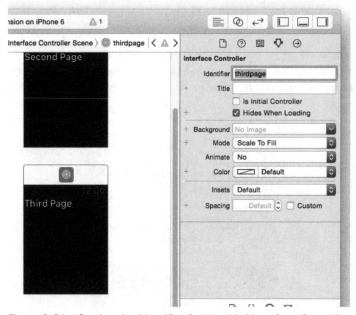

Figure 2.31   Setting the Identifier for the third Interface Controller

4. Run the application on the iPhone 6 Simulator and click the **Display Screen** button on the Apple Watch simulator. This time, you see that the second

Interface Controller is displayed with two dots at the bottom of the screen. Swiping from right to left reveals the third Interface Controller (see Figure 2.32).

Figure 2.32   The user can slide between the two Interface Controllers

Changing the Current Page to Display

In the previous section, you saw that you could display a series of Interface Controllers that the user can swipe through. What if you want to programmatically jump to a particular page? In this case, what if you want to display the Third Page instead of the Second Page? Let's see how this can be done.

1. Add two `WKInterfaceController` classes to the NavigateUsingCode WatchKit Extension group of the project and name them **SecondInterfaceController.swift** and **ThirdInterfaceController.swift**, respectively. Figure 2.33 shows the location of the files.

Figure 2.33   Adding the two Swift files to the project

2. Populate the SecondInterfaceController.swift file as follows:

```swift
import WatchKit
import Foundation

class SecondInterfaceController: WKInterfaceController {

    override func awakeWithContext(context: AnyObject?) {
        super.awakeWithContext(context)

        // Configure interface objects here.
        println("SecondInterfaceController - awakeWithContext")
    }

    override func willActivate() {
        // This method is called when watch view controller is about to be
        // visible to user
        super.willActivate()
        println("SecondInterfaceController - willActivate")
    }

    override func didDeactivate() {
        // This method is called when watch view controller is no longer
        // visible
        super.didDeactivate()
        println("SecondInterfaceController - didDeactivate")
    }

}
```

3. Populate the ThirdInterfaceController.swift file as follows:

```swift
import WatchKit
import Foundation

class ThirdInterfaceController: WKInterfaceController {

    override func awakeWithContext(context: AnyObject?) {
        super.awakeWithContext(context)

        // Configure interface objects here.
        println("ThirdInterfaceController - awakeWithContext")
    }

    override func willActivate() {
        // This method is called when watch view controller is about to be
        // visible to user
        super.willActivate()
```

```
        println("ThirdInterfaceController - willActivate")
    }

    override func didDeactivate() {
        // This method is called when watch view controller is no longer
        // visible
        super.didDeactivate()
        println("ThirdInterfaceController - didDeactivate")
    }

}
```

4. In the Interface.storyboard file, set the Class property of the second Interface Controller to **SecondInterfaceController** (see Figure 2.34). Likewise, set the Class property of the third Interface Controller to **ThirdInterfaceController**.

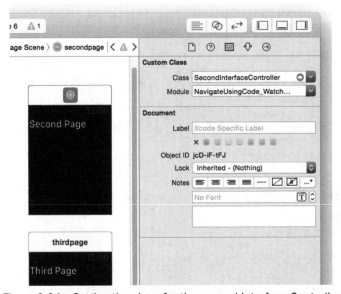

Figure 2.34   Setting the class for the second Interface Controller

5. Run the application on the iPhone 6 Simulator and click the **Display Screen** button on the Apple Watch simulator. Observe the statements printed in the Output window (see Figure 2.35). As you can see, the awakeWithContext method is fired for both the second and third Interface Controllers, even though only the second Interface Controller is visible initially.

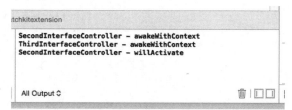

Figure 2.35   Both Interface Controllers fire the awakeWithContext method

6. If you want the third Interface Controller to load instead of the second, you can use the becomeCurrentPage method. Calling this method in an Interface Controller brings it into view. Because both the second and third Interface Controllers fire the awakeWithContext method when you click the **Display Screen** button, you can call the becomeCurrentPage method in the awakeWithContext method. Hence, add the following statement in bold to the ThirdInterfaceController.swift file:

```
override func awakeWithContext(context: AnyObject?) {
    super.awakeWithContext(context)

    // Configure interface objects here.
    becomeCurrentPage()
    println("ThirdInterfaceController - awakeWithContext")
}
```

7. Run the application on the iPhone 6 Simulator and click the **Display Screen** button on the Apple Watch simulator. This time, you see that after the second Interface Controller is displayed, it will automatically scroll to the third one.

Summary

In this chapter, you delved deeper into how Interface Controllers work in your Apple Watch application. You learned

- The lifecycle of an Interface Controller
- How to navigate between Interface Controllers
- The different methods of displaying an Interface Controller
- How to programmatically display an Interface Controller
- How to display a series of Interface Controllers

Apple Watch User Interface

If you haven't found it yet, keep looking. Don't settle. As with all matters of the heart, you'll know when you find it. And like any great relationship, it just gets better and better as the years roll on.

Steve Jobs

Designing the user interface (UI) for your Apple Watch application is similar to designing for the iPhone. However, space is at a premium on the Apple Watch, and every millimeter on the screen must be put to good use in order to convey the exact intention of your app.

The UI of an Apple Watch application is represented by various controls (commonly known as *views* in iOS programming), and they are divided into two main categories:

- **Responding to user interactions**: Users directly interact with these controls to perform some actions. Examples of such controls are Button, Switch, Slider, and Table.
- **Displaying information**: These controls mainly display information to the user. Examples of such controls are Label, Images, and Table.

In this and the next chapter, you learn how to use these various controls to build the UI of your application.

Responding to User Interactions

One key way to interact with the Apple Watch is to use the tap gesture. You can tap the following controls:

- Button
- Switch
- Slider
- Table

Let's take a more detailed look at these objects!

> **Note**
>
> I cover the Table control later in this chapter when we discuss controls that display information.

Button

The Button control is the most direct way of interacting with an Apple Watch application. A Button can display text as well as a background image. Tapping a Button triggers an action on the Interface Controller where you can write the code to perform the appropriate action.

Adding a Button to an Interface Controller

In this section, you will create a project that that uses a Button. Subsequent sections will show you how to customize the button by creating an action for it and then displaying its title using custom fonts.

1. Using Xcode, create a new Single View Application project and name it **Buttons**.
2. Add a WatchKit App target to the project. Uncheck the option Include Notification Scene so that we can keep the WatchKit project to a bare minimum.
3. Select the Interface.storyboard file to edit it in the Storyboard Editor.
4. Drag and drop a Button control onto the storyboard, as shown in Figure 3.1.

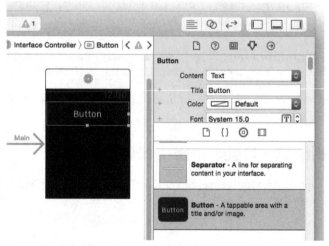

Figure 3.1   Adding a Button control to the Interface Controller

5. In the Attributes Inspector window, set the Title attribute to **Play** (see Figure 3.2).

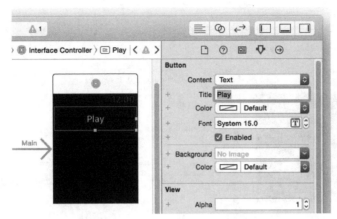

Figure 3.2   Changing the title of the Button

6. Run the application on to the iPhone 6 Simulator. You should see the button on the Apple Watch Simulator (see Figure 3.3). You can click it (or tap it on a real Apple Watch).

Figure 3.3   Testing the Button on the Apple Watch Simulator

Creating an Action for a Button

For the Button control to do anything useful, you need to create an action for it so that when the user taps it, your application can perform some actions. To create this action, follow these steps:

1. In the Storyboard Editor, select the **View | Assistant Editor | Show Assistant Editor** menu item to show the InterfaceController.swift file.

2. Control-click the Button control in the Interface Controller and drag and drop it over the InterfaceController class (see Figure 3.4).

Figure 3.4   Creating an action for the Button

3. Create an Action for the Button and name it **btnPlay** (see Figure 3.5). Click **Connect**.

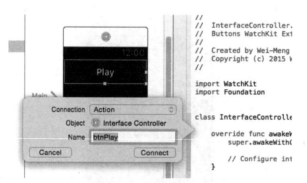

Figure 3.5   Naming the action

4. You now see the action created in the InterfaceController.swift file:

```
import WatchKit
import Foundation

class InterfaceController: WKInterfaceController {

    @IBAction func btnPlay() {
    }
```

5. Add the following statement in bold to the InterfaceController.swift file:

```
@IBAction func btnPlay() {
    println("The button was tapped!")
}
```

6. Run the application on the iPhone 6 Simulator. Click the **Play** button and observe the statement printed in the Output window (see Figure 3.6).

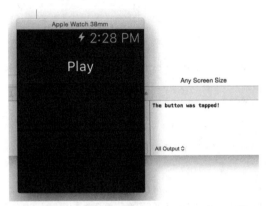

Figure 3.6   Clicking the Button fires the action

Creating an Outlet for a Button

You can also programmatically change the title of the Button control during runtime. To do so, you need to create an outlet for the Button:

1. With the Assistant Editor shown, control-click the Button and drag and drop it over the InterfaceController.swift file. Name the outlet **button1** (see Figure 3.7) and click **Connect**.

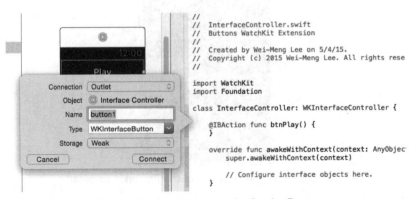

Figure 3.7   Creating an outlet for the Button

2. This creates an outlet in the InterfaceController.swift file:

```
import WatchKit
import Foundation

class InterfaceController: WKInterfaceController {

    @IBOutlet weak var button1: WKInterfaceButton!

    @IBAction func btnPlay() {
        println("The button was tapped!")
    }
```

3. Add the following statements in bold to the InterfaceController.swift file:

```
override func awakeWithContext(context: AnyObject?) {
    super.awakeWithContext(context)

    // Configure interface objects here.
    button1.setTitle("Play Video")
}
```

> **Note**
>
> Observe that, while you can change the title of a Button, you cannot get the title of the Button programmatically. For efficiency and battery preservation, getting the title from the Button requires a round trip to the watch and back to the extension again. Hence, the WatchKit API does not allow you to do that. You are required to maintain the state of your UI yourself.

4. Run the application on the iPhone 6 Simulator. You should now see the title of the Button changed to Play Video (see Figure 3.8).

Figure 3.8   Changing the title of the Button dynamically

Displaying Attributed Strings

The Button control supports *attributed strings*. Attributed strings allow you to specify different attributes (such as color, font, size, etc.) for different parts of a string. In the following steps, you will display the title of the Button using different colors.

1. Add the following statements in bold to the InterfaceController.swift file:

```
override func awakeWithContext(context: AnyObject?) {
    super.awakeWithContext(context)

    // Configure interface objects here.
    //button1.setTitle("Play Video")

    var str = NSMutableAttributedString(string: "Hello, Apple Watch!")

    //------display the Hello in yellow---
    str.addAttribute(NSForegroundColorAttributeName,
        value: UIColor.yellowColor(),
        range: NSMakeRange(0, 5))

    //---display the , in red---
    str.addAttribute(NSForegroundColorAttributeName,
        value: UIColor.redColor(),
        range: NSMakeRange(5, 1))

    //---display Apple Watch! in green---
    str.addAttribute(NSForegroundColorAttributeName,
        value: UIColor.greenColor(),
        range: NSMakeRange(7, 12))
    button1.setAttributedTitle(str)
}
```

2. Run the application on the iPhone 6 Simulator. You should see the title of the Button displayed in multiple colors, as shown in Figure 3.9.

Figure 3.9 Displaying the Button title with mixed colors

Using Custom Fonts

Using attributed strings, you can also use different fonts for parts of a string. To illustrate this, let's modify the example in the previous section to display part of the Button's title using a custom font.

For this example, use the Impact font that is installed on your Mac. The Impact font is represented using the Impact.ttf file located in the /Library/Fonts/ folder on your Mac.

1. Drag and drop a copy of the Impact.ttf file onto the extension target of the project in Xcode.

2. You are asked to choose a few options. Select the options shown in Figure 3.10. This adds the Impact.ttf file onto the Extension and WatchKit App targets of the project.

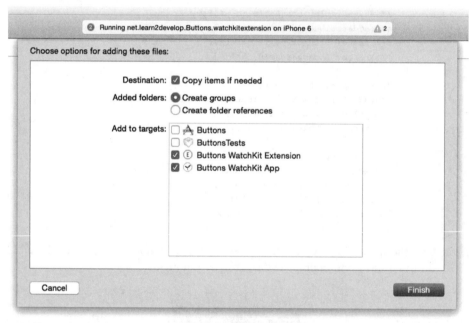

Figure 3.10   Adding the font file to the Extension and the WatchKit App targets

> **Note**
>
> Remember to add the font file to both the WatchKit Extension and WatchKit App. Also, be aware that adding custom fonts to the project adds considerable size and memory usage on your watch app. So, try to use the system font unless you have a very good reason not to.

3. Figure 3.11 shows the Impact.ttf file in the project.

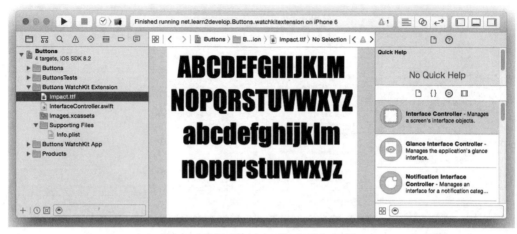

Figure 3.11   The font file in the project

4. Add a new key named **UIAppFonts** to the Info.plist file located in the extension target and set its Item 0 to **Impact.ttf** (see Figure 3.12).

> **Note**
>
> If your Info.plist file is not showing the items as shown in Figure 3.12, simply right-click any of the items in it and select **Show Raw Keys/Values**.

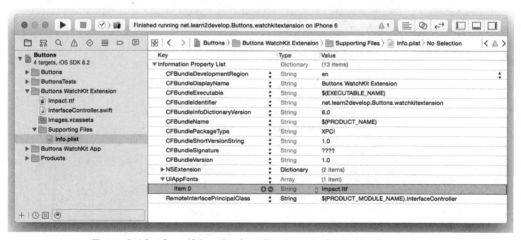

Figure 3.12   Specifying the font filename in the extension project

5. Likewise, add a new key named **UIAppFonts** to the Info.plist file located in the WatchKit App target and set its Item 0 to **Impact.ttf** (see Figure 3.13).

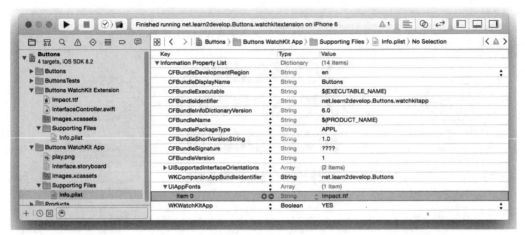

Figure 3.13   Specifying the font filename in the WatchKit app project

6. Add the following statements in bold to the InterfaceController.swift file:

```
override func awakeWithContext(context: AnyObject?) {
    super.awakeWithContext(context)

    // Configure interface objects here.
    //button1.setTitle("Play Video")

    var str = NSMutableAttributedString(string: "Hello, Apple Watch!")
    //------display the Hello in yellow---
    str.addAttribute(NSForegroundColorAttributeName,
        value: UIColor.yellowColor(),
        range: NSMakeRange(0, 5))

    //---display Hello using the Impact font, size 22---
    str.addAttribute(NSFontAttributeName,
        value: UIFont(name: "Impact", size: 22.0)!,
        range: NSMakeRange(0, 5))

    //---display the , in red---
    str.addAttribute(NSForegroundColorAttributeName,
        value: UIColor.redColor(),
        range: NSMakeRange(5, 1))

    //---display Apple Watch! in green---
    str.addAttribute(NSForegroundColorAttributeName,
        value: UIColor.greenColor(),
        range: NSMakeRange(7, 12))

    button1.setAttributedTitle(str)
}
```

7. Run the application on the iPhone 6 Simulator. You should now see "Hello" displayed using the Impact font (see Figure 3.14).

Figure 3.14   Displaying "Hello" using custom font

Note

Once you have added a custom font to your project, you can also use the font directly in Interface Builder by changing the Font attribute of a control and setting it to **Custom** and then selecting the font that you want to use in the Family attribute.

Getting the Font Name

One common problem in dealing with fonts is that the filename of the custom font that you are using is not always the same as the font name. The following code snippet allows you to print out the name of each font family and their corresponding font names:

```
for family in UIFont.familyNames() {
    println(family)
    for name in UIFont.fontNamesForFamilyName(family as String) {
        println("--\(name)")
    }
}
```

The previous code snippet prints out the output, as shown in Figure 3.15. For example, if you want to use the Helvetica Neue font, you have to specify in your code one of the font names printed: HelveticaNeue-Italic, HelveticaNeue-Bold, etc.

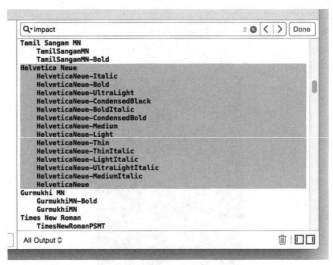

Figure 3.15   Printing out the font families and their associated font names

Changing Background Image of Button

Besides displaying text, the Button control can also display a background image. The following exercise will show you how to add an image to the project and use it as the background of a button.

1. Drag and drop an image named play.png onto the Images.xcassets items in the WatchKit App target (see Figure 3.16, top).

> **Note**
>
> You can find a copy of this image in the source code download for this book.

2. As the Apple Watch has a Retina display, move the icon to the box labeled **2×** (see Figure 3.16, bottom).

3. If you want to use different images for the 38mm Apple Watch and the 42mm Apple Watch, you can select the **play** icon in the Images.xcassets file and view its Attributes Inspector window. Then, for the Devices attribute, select **Device Specific** (see Figure 3.17, top). You can now drag and drop the images you want to use onto the boxes labeled "38 mm 2×" and "42 mm 2×" (see Figure 3.17, bottom). For this example, you will use the same image for the two different watch sizes.

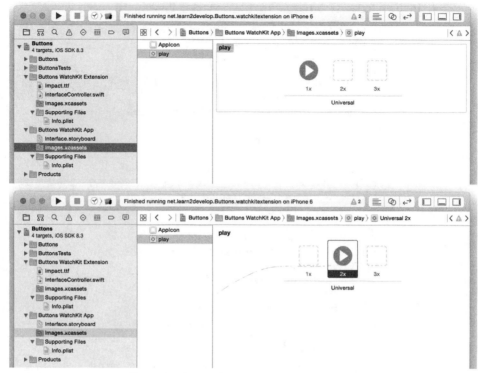

Figure 3.16   Adding an image to the project

Figure 3.17   Specifying device-specific images to use

4. In the InterfaceController.swift file, add the following statements in bold:

```
override func awakeWithContext(context: AnyObject?) {
    super.awakeWithContext(context)
    // Configure interface objects here.
    /*
    var str = NSMutableAttributedString(string: "Hello, Apple Watch!")
    //------display the Hello in yellow---
    str.addAttribute(NSForegroundColorAttributeName,
        value: UIColor.yellowColor(),
        range: NSMakeRange(0, 5))

    //---display Hello using the Impact font, size 22---
    str.addAttribute(NSFontAttributeName,
        value: UIFont(name: "Impact", size: 22.0)!,
        range: NSMakeRange(0, 5))

    //---display the , in red---
    str.addAttribute(NSForegroundColorAttributeName,
        value: UIColor.redColor(),
        range: NSMakeRange(5, 1))

    //---display Apple Watch! in green---
    str.addAttribute(NSForegroundColorAttributeName,
        value: UIColor.greenColor(),
        range: NSMakeRange(7, 12))

    button1.setAttributedTitle(str)
    */

    button1.setBackgroundImageNamed("play")
}
```

5. Run the application on the iPhone 6 Simulator. You should now see the image on the button on the Apple Watch Simulator (see Figure 3.18).

Figure 3.18   Displaying an image on the Button

Do not use the `setBackgroundImage:` method by passing it an `UIImage` instance, like this:

```
button1.setBackgroundImage(UIImage(named: "play"))
```

This is because the `UIImage` class looks for the specified image ("play") in the main bundle. And because the play.png file is in the WatchKit App target, the image cannot be found and hence the image will not be set successfully.

6. You can set the background image of the Button in Storyboard via the Background attribute in the Attributes Inspector window.

Switch

The Switch control allows the user to toggle between the ON and OFF states. It is commonly used in cases where you allow users to enable or disable a particular setting. In the following example, you will create a project and see how the Switch control works.

1. Using Xcode, create a new Single View Application project and name it **Switches**.

2. Add a WatchKit App target to the project. Uncheck the option Include Notification Scene so that we can keep the WatchKit project to a bare minimum.

3. Select the Interface.storyboard to edit it in the Storyboard Editor.

4. Drag and drop a Switch control onto the default Interface Controller (see Figure 3.19).

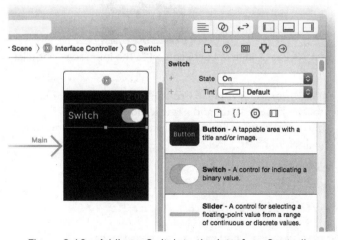

Figure 3.19   Adding a Switch to the Interface Controller

5. In the Attributes Inspector window, set the Title attribute of the Switch control to **Aircon** (see Figure 3.20).

Figure 3.20   Changing the title of the Switch control

6. Add a Label control to the Interface Controller (see Figure 3.21).

Figure 3.21   Adding a Label control to the Interface Controller

7. Create an outlet for the Switch control and name it **switch**. Likewise, create
   an outlet for the Label control and name it **label**. Then, create an action for the
   Switch control and name it **switchAction**. The InterfaceController.swift file
   should now look like this:

```
import WatchKit
import Foundation

class InterfaceController: WKInterfaceController {

    @IBOutlet weak var `switch`: WKInterfaceSwitch!

    @IBOutlet weak var label: WKInterfaceLabel!

    @IBAction func switchAction(value: Bool) {
    }
```

> **Note**
>
> Because `switch` is a reserved word in the Swift programming language, if you try to use it as the name of an outlet, you have to enclose it with a pair of back quotes (`` `` ``).

8. Add the following statements in bold to the InterfaceController.swift file:

```
@IBAction func switchAction(value: Bool) {
    value ? label.setText("Aircon is on") :
        label.setText("Aircon is off")
}

override func awakeWithContext(context: AnyObject?) {
    super.awakeWithContext(context)

    // Configure interface objects here.
    `switch`.setOn(false)
    label.setText("")
}
```

> **Note**
>
> You can programmatically set the value of a Switch control, but you will not be able to get its value. To know its value, you need to implement the action of the Switch control and save its value whenever its state changes.

9. Run the application on the iPhone 6 Simulator. On the Apple Watch Simulator, click the **Switch** control to turn it on and off and observe the message printed in the Label control (see Figure 3.22).

Figure 3.22   Testing the Switch control

Slider

The Slider is a visual control with two buttons (– and +) that allows the user to decrement or increment a floating point value. It is usually used in situations where you want the user to select from a range of values, such as the temperature settings in a thermostat.

1. Using Xcode, create a new Single View Application project and name it **Sliders**.
2. Add a WatchKit App target to the project. Uncheck the option Include Notification Scene so that we can keep the WatchKit project to a bare minimum.
3. Select the Interface.storyboard to edit it in the Storyboard Editor.
4. Drag and drop a Slider control onto the default Interface Controller (see Figure 3.23).

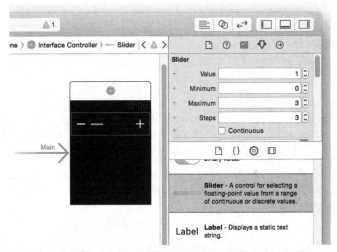

Figure 3.23   Adding a Slider to the Interface Controller

5. Run the application on the iPhone 6 Simulator. On the Apple Watch Simulator, click the **+** and **–** buttons (see Figure 3.24) and observe the Slider.

Figure 3.24   Testing the Slider

6. Add a Label control to the Interface Controller (see Figure 3.25).

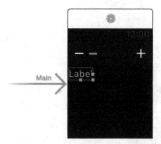

Figure 3.25   Adding a Label to the Interface Controller

7. Create an outlet for the Slider control and name it **slider**. Likewise, create an outlet for the Label control and name it **label**. Then, create an action for the Slider control and name it **sliderAction**. The InterfaceController.swift file should now look like this:

```
import WatchKit
import Foundation

class InterfaceController: WKInterfaceController {

    @IBOutlet weak var label: WKInterfaceLabel!

    @IBOutlet weak var slider: WKInterfaceSlider!

    @IBAction func sliderAction(value: Float) {
    }
```

8. Set the following attributes for the Slider control as follows (see Figure 3.26):

   a. Maximum: **10**

   b. Steps: **5**

9. Add the following statements in bold to the InterfaceController.swift file:

```
    @IBAction func sliderAction(value: Float) {
        label.setText("\(value)")
    }

    override func awakeWithContext(context: AnyObject?) {
        super.awakeWithContext(context)

        // Configure interface objects here.
        slider.setValue(0.0)
        label.setText("0.0")
    }
```

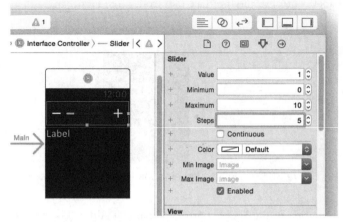

Figure 3.26   Setting the attributes for the Slider control

> **Note**
>
> You can programmatically set the value of a Slider control, but you will not be able to get its value. To know its value, you need to implement the action of the Slider control and save its value whenever its value changes.

10. Run the application on the iPhone 6 Simulator. Click the – and + buttons and observe the value printed on the Label control (see Figure 3.27).

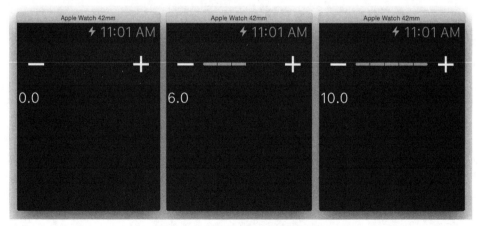

Figure 3.27   Testing the Slider

The Steps attribute specifies how many times you can click the Slider to reach its maximum value. The increment or decrement value of the Slider at any point is dependent on the length of the Slider (Maximum value minus the Minimum value) divided by the value of Steps. In this example, the length of the Slider is 10 (maximum of 10 minus minimum of 0) and the value of Steps is five; hence, the Slider increments or decrements by 2 whenever the **+** or **–** button is clicked.

Displaying Information

To display information to the user on the Apple Watch, the WatchKit provides the following controls:

- **Label**: A control that displays formatted texts and the content of which can be changed dynamically.
- **Image**: A control that displays a single image or a series of images (for animation).
- **Table**: A control that displays a list of data. Only single-column tables are supported at this moment.

Labels

Until this point, you have been using the Label object in a number of projects. As you have seen, the Label control displays a string of text. Like the Button control, the Label also supports attributed strings.

> **Note**
>
> Refer to the earlier section, "Displaying Attributed Strings," for more information on attributed strings.

We discuss more about the Label control in Chapter 4, "Interfacing with iOS Apps," where you learn about the strategy to internationalize and localize your Apple Watch applications.

Images

You can use images in several places:

- As the background of an Interface Controller
- As the background of a Button (discussed in the section on Buttons)
- Independently using the Image control

Setting the Background of an Interface Controller

Let's first learn how to change the background of the Interface Controller to display an image.

1. Using Xcode, create a new Single View Application project and name it **Images**.
2. Add a WatchKit App target to the project. Uncheck the option Include Notification Scene so that we can keep the WatchKit project to a bare minimum.

3. Drag and drop two images named flag.png and apple.png to the Images.xcassets file in the WatchKit App target of the project (see Figure 3.28).

> **Note**
>
> You can find a copy of the images in the source code download for this book.

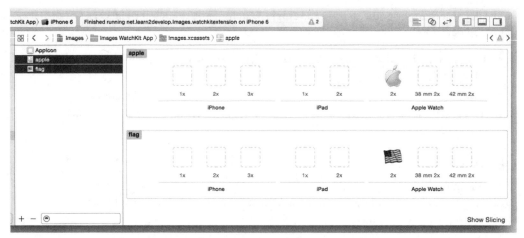

Figure 3.28   Adding an image to the project

4. Select the Interface.storyboard to edit it in the Storyboard Editor.
5. In the default Interface Controller, set the Background attribute to **apple** (see Figure 3.29) and set its Mode attribute to **Aspect Fit**. The image will be displayed as the background for the Interface Controller.

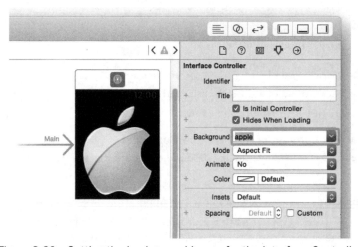

Figure 3.29   Setting the background image for the Interface Controller

6. Run the application on the iPhone 6 Simulator. You should see the Apple Simulator showing the image (see Figure 3.30).

Figure 3.30   The Interface Controller showing the image in the background

Using the Image Control

The previous section showed how the Interface Controller could display an image as its background. In this section, you will learn how to use the Image control to display an image on the Interface Controller.

1. Using the same project created in the previous section, add an Image control onto the Interface Controller (see Figure 3.31). Set its Horizontal and Vertical attributes to **Center**.

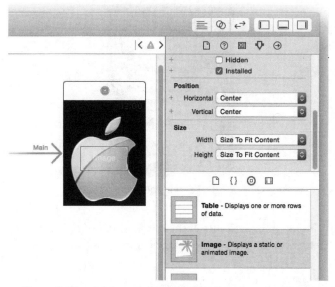

Figure 3.31   Adding an Image to the Interface Controller

2. Set its Image attribute to **flag** (see Figure 3.32) and Mode attribute to **Scale to Fill**.

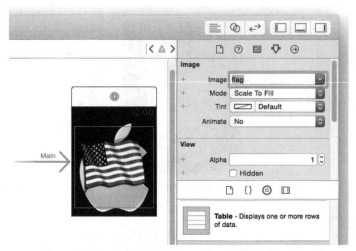

Figure 3.32   Setting the image for the Image control

3. Run the application on the iPhone 6 Simulator. You should see the Apple Simulator showing the image (see Figure 3.33).

Figure 3.33   Testing the Image control

4. You can also programmatically set the image in the Image control using the `setImageNamed:` method of the Image control. To do that, create an outlet

for the Image control and add the following statements in bold to the InterfaceController.swift file:

```
import WatchKit
import Foundation

class InterfaceController: WKInterfaceController {

    @IBOutlet weak var image: WKInterfaceImage!

    override func awakeWithContext(context: AnyObject?) {
        super.awakeWithContext(context)

        // Configure interface objects here.
        image.setImageNamed("flag")
    }
```

> **Note**
>
> For this step, you need to clear the Image attribute for the Image control, which was previously set to **flag** in Step 2.

Performing Animation

In the Apple Watch, animations are performed using a series of static images. These images are stored in the WatchKit app bundle so that they can be presented quickly to the user. In this section, you learn how to perform simple animations using the Image control:

1. Using the same project created in the previous section, drag and drop a series of images to the Images.xcassets file in the WatchKit App target (see Figure 3.34).

   > **Note**
   >
   > You can find a copy of the images in the source code download for this book.

   The images should be named and sized as follows:

Image Name	Size
heart0.png	130x113 pixels
heart1.png	110x96 pixels
heart2.png	90x78 pixels
heart3.png	70x61 pixels
heart4.png	50x43 pixels

Figure 3.34   Adding the series of images for the animation

2. Set the Mode attribute of the Image control in the Interface Controller to **Center** (see Figure 3.35).

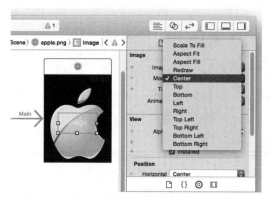

Figure 3.35   Setting the display mode for the Image control

3. Add the following statements in bold to the InterfaceController.swift file:

```
override func awakeWithContext(context: AnyObject?) {
    super.awakeWithContext(context)

    // Configure interface objects here.
    image.setImageNamed("heart")

    //---use 5 images, change every 0.5 seconds,
    //---location is the starting image - 0 for heart0.png, length is
    // for number of images to animate---
    image.startAnimatingWithImagesInRange(
        NSRange(location:0, length:5),
        duration: 0.5, repeatCount: Int.max)
}
```

4. Run the application on the iPhone 6 Simulator. You should see a throbbing heart (see Figure 3.36).

Figure 3.36   The animation of the throbbing heart

Table

In an Apple Watch application, you use a Table control to display a list of items. For example, you might want to display a list of names on your Apple Watch. Tables are not limited to displaying text; you can also display images on each row. In fact, each row can be configured to display a combination of the different controls that we cover in this chapter.

1. Using Xcode, create a new Single View Application project and name it **Tables**.

2. Add a WatchKit App target to the project. Uncheck the option Include Notification Scene so that we can keep the WatchKit project to a bare minimum.

3. Select the Interface.storyboard file located in the Tables WatchKit App target to edit it in the Storyboard Editor.

4. Add a Table control to the Interface Controller (see Figure 3.37).

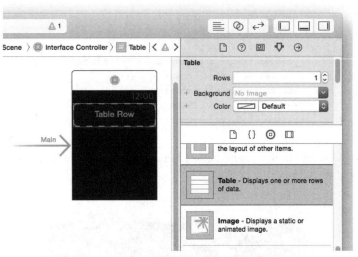

Figure 3.37   Adding a Table to the Interface Controller

5. Add a Label control onto the Table control, as shown in Figure 3.38.

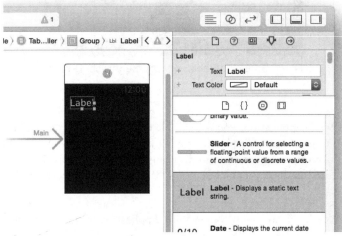

Figure 3.38   Adding a Label onto the Table control

6. Select the Label control and set its Horizontal and Vertical attributes to **Center** (see Figure 3.39). This makes the Label control appear in the center of the Table control.

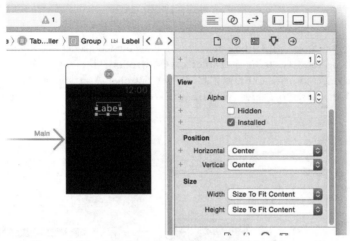

Figure 3.39   Setting the attributes for the Label control

7. Add a Swift file (**iOS | Swift File**) to the Extension target of the project and name it **FruitsTableRowController.swift** (see Figure 3.40).

Figure 3.40   Adding a Swift class to the project

8. Populate the FruitsTableRowController.swift file with the following:

```
import UIKit
import WatchKit

class FruitsTableRowController: NSObject {
    @IBOutlet weak var label: WKInterfaceLabel!
}
```

9. Back in the Storyboard Editor, select the Table Row Controller (see Figure 3.41, top) and then set its Class to **FruitsTableRowController**. The Table Row Controller now changes its name to Fruits Table Row Controller. Also, you need to ensure that the Module is set to **Tables_WatchKit_Extension** (see Figure 3.41, bottom).

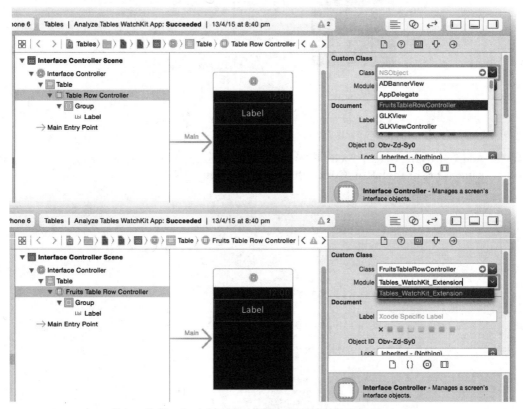

Figure 3.41   Assigning the Table control to the Swift class

10. Select the Fruits Table Row Controller and then set its Identifier attribute to **FruitsTableRowControllerID** (see Figure 3.42). The Fruits Table Row Controller now changes its name to FruitsTableRowControllerID.

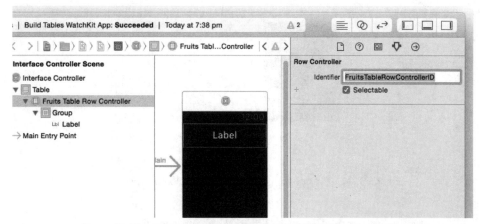

Figure 3.42   Setting the Identifier for the Table Row Controller

11. Right-click **FruitsTableRowControllerID** and, in the popup, connect the label outlet to the Label control on the Table (see Figure 3.43).

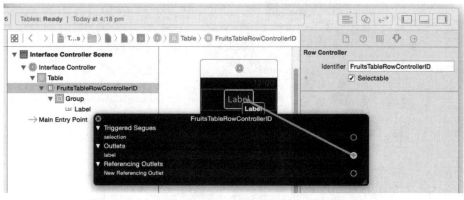

Figure 3.43   Connecting the outlet to the Label control

12. Click the **View | Assistant Editor | Show Assistant Editor** menu item to reveal the code editor. Control-click the **Table** control (see Figure 3.44) and drag and drop it over the InterfaceController class.

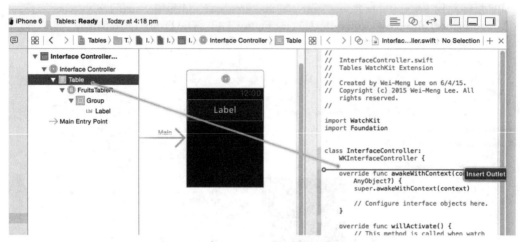

Figure 3.44 Creating an outlet for the Table control

13. Name the outlet **tableView** (see Figure 3.45) and click **Connect**.

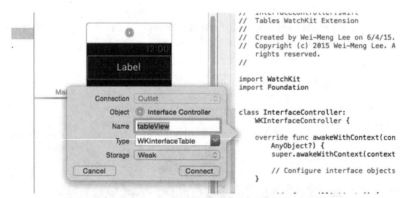

Figure 3.45 Naming the outlet

14. Add the following statements in bold to the InterfaceController.swift file:

```
import WatchKit
import Foundation

class InterfaceController: WKInterfaceController {

    @IBOutlet weak var tableView: WKInterfaceTable!
```

```
var fruits = [
    "Durian",
    "Pineapple",
    "Apple",
    "Orange",
    "Guava",
    "Peach",
    "Rambutan" ]

func populateTableView() {
    tableView.setNumberOfRows(fruits.count,
        withRowType: "FruitsTableRowControllerID")

    for (index, value) in enumerate(fruits) {
        let row = tableView.rowControllerAtIndex(index) as!
            FruitsTableRowController
        row.label.setText(value)
    }
}

override func awakeWithContext(context: AnyObject?) {
    super.awakeWithContext(context)

    // Configure interface objects here.
    populateTableView()
}
```

15. Run the application on the iPhone 6 Simulator. You should now see a list of fruits shown on the Apple Watch Simulator (see Figure 3.46).

Figure 3.46   The Table control displaying a list of items

Displaying Images

Besides displaying text in the Table control, it is often more useful to display images next to the text.

1. Add an image named fruit.png to the Images.xcassets file in the WatchKit App target of the project (see Figure 3.47).

   > **Note**
   > You can find a copy of the images in the source code download for this book.

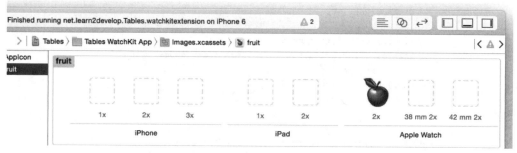

Figure 3.47   Adding an image to the project

2. Add an Image control onto the Table control, as shown in Figure 3.48.

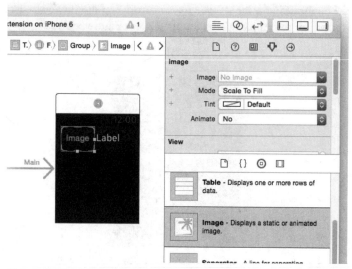

Figure 3.48   Adding an Image control to the Table Row Controller

3. Set the attributes of the Image control as follows (see Figure 3.49):

   a. Mode: **Aspect Fill**

   b. Horizontal: **Right**

   c. Vertical: **Center**

   d. Width: **30**

   e. Height: **30**

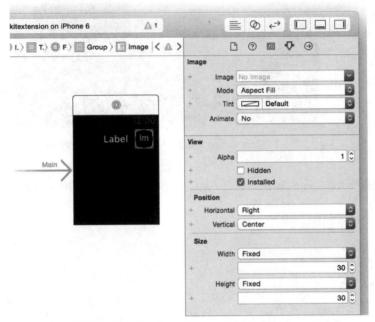

Figure 3.49   Setting the attributes for the Image control

4. Add the following statement in bold to the FruitsTableRowController.swift file:

```
import UIKit
import WatchKit

class FruitsTableRowController: NSObject {
    @IBOutlet weak var label: WKInterfaceLabel!
    @IBOutlet weak var image: WKInterfaceImage!
}
```

5. Back in the Storyboard Editor, right-click **FruitsTableRowControllerID** and connect the image outlet to the Image control (see Figure 3.50).

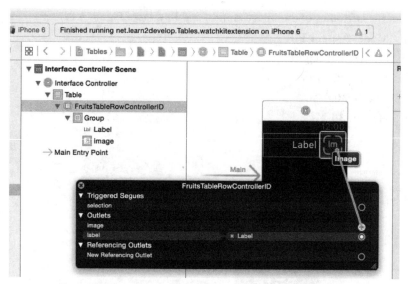

Figure 3.50   Connecting the outlet to the Image control

6. Add the following statements in bold to the InterfaceController.swift file:

```swift
import WatchKit
import Foundation

class InterfaceController: WKInterfaceController {

    @IBOutlet weak var tableView: WKInterfaceTable!

    var fruits = [
        "Durian",
        "Pineapple",
        "Apple",
        "Orange",
        "Guava",
        "Peach",
        "Rambutan" ]

    func populateTableView() {
        tableView.setNumberOfRows(fruits.count,
            withRowType: "FruitsTableRowControllerID")

        for (index, value) in enumerate(fruits) {
            let row = tableView.rowControllerAtIndex(index) as!
                FruitsTableRowController
```

```
        row.label.setText(value)
        row.image.setImageNamed("fruit")
    }
}
```

7. Run the application on the iPhone 6 Simulator. You see the image displayed next to each row in the Table control (see Figure 3.51).

Figure 3.51   The Table control with the images displayed for each row

Selecting an Item in a Table

When an item in the Table control is tapped, the `table:didSelectRowAtIndex:` method will fire.

> **Note**
>
> If you simply want to use the Table control to display a list of information and not make the individual rows tappable, uncheck the Selectable attribute of the Row Controller as shown in Figure 3.42.

You simply need to implement this method if you want to perform an action when an item is selected, such as navigating to another Interface Controller.

1. Add the following statements in bold to the InterfaceController.swift file:

```
class InterfaceController: WKInterfaceController {

    @IBOutlet weak var tableView: WKInterfaceTable!

    var fruits = [
        "Durian",
        "Pineapple",
        "Apple",
        "Orange",
```

```
    "Guava",
    "Peach",
    "Rambutan" ]

override func table(table: WKInterfaceTable,
    didSelectRowAtIndex rowIndex: Int) {
    println(fruits[rowIndex])
}
```

2. Run the application on the iPhone 6 Simulator. Click an item and observe that the Output window displays the name of the fruit selected (see Figure 3.52).

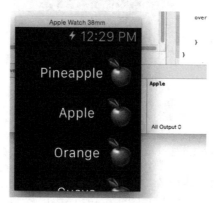

Figure 3.52   Clicking a row displays the name of the item

Gathering Information

While the Apple Watch is more for consuming information, there are certainly times where it is necessary to obtain inputs from the users. Users can use the following methods to provide inputs:

- Selecting from a predefined list of text
- Voice dictation
- Selecting from a list of emojis

Getting Text Inputs

Getting text inputs from the Apple Watch is done through the `presentTextInput-ControllerWithSuggestions:allowedInputMode:completion:` method. This method presents an interface that can accept user inputs by showing the user a list of predefined texts, obtaining inputs through dictation, or selecting an emoji.

In the following exercise, you will learn how to obtain text (as well as emojis) from the user.

1. Using Xcode, create a new Single View Application project and name it **TextInputs**.

2. Add a WatchKit App target to the project. Uncheck the option Include Notification Scene so that we can keep the WatchKit project to a bare minimum.

3. Select the Interface.storyboard to edit it in the Storyboard Editor.

4. Drag and drop a Button and a Label control onto the default Interface Controller (see Figure 3.53). Set the title of the Button to "Select Symbol," as shown.

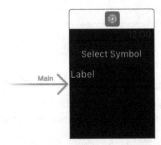

Figure 3.53   Adding the Button and the Label controls to the Interface Controller

5. Create an action for the Button and name it **btnSelectSymbol**, and create an outlet for the Label control and name it **lblSymbolSelected** in the InterfaceController .swift file:

```
import WatchKit
import Foundation

class InterfaceController: WKInterfaceController {

    @IBAction func btnSelectSymbol() {
    }

    @IBOutlet weak var lblSymbolSelected: WKInterfaceLabel!
```

6. Add the following statements in bold to the InterfaceController.swift file:

```
import WatchKit
import Foundation

class InterfaceController: WKInterfaceController {

    @IBAction func btnSelectSymbol() {
        presentTextInputControllerWithSuggestions(
            ["AAPL", "AMZN", "FB", "GOOG"],
            allowedInputMode: WKTextInputMode.Plain)
            { (results) -> Void in
                if results != nil {
```

```
                          //---trying to see if the result can be converted to
                          // String---
                          var symbol = results.first as? String
                          if symbol != nil {
                              self.lblSymbolSelected.setText("Symbol: " + symbol!)
                          }
                      }
                  }
          }

          @IBOutlet weak var lblSymbolSelected: WKInterfaceLabel!

          override func awakeWithContext(context: AnyObject?) {
              super.awakeWithContext(context)

              // Configure interface objects here.
              lblSymbolSelected.setText("")
          }
```

The `presentTextInputControllerWithSuggestions:allowedInputMode:`
`completion:` method takes in two arguments and a closure:

- An array of strings containing suggestions for the user to select.
- The input mode: plain text, emoji, or animated emoji.
- A block to execute after the user has dismissed the modal interface. The result
  is an array containing the input by the user. If the user has input a string, the
  array contains an `NSString` object. If the user inputs an emoji, the array will
  contain an `NSData` object.

For this example, you ask the user to input plain text.

7. Run the application on the iPhone Simulator and click **Select Symbol** on the
   Apple Watch Simulator (see Figure 3.54). You will be able to select from a list
   of predefined symbols. You can also tap the microphone button to use the Apple
   Watch's dictation capability to get text inputs.

Figure 3.54   Testing the application

> **Note**
> The Apple Watch Simulator does not support dictation.

Getting Emojis

As described in the previous section, the `presentTextInputControllerWith-Suggestions:allowedInputMode:completion:` method can also accept emojis or animated emojis. To get emojis, follow these steps:

1. Add the following statements in bold to the InterfaceController.swift file:

```
@IBAction func btnSelectSymbol() {
    presentTextInputControllerWithSuggestions(
        ["AAPL", "AMZN", "FB", "GOOG"],
        allowedInputMode: WKTextInputMode.AllowEmoji)
        { (results) -> Void in
            if results != nil {
                //---trying to see if the result can be converted
                // to String---
                var symbol = results.first as? String
                if symbol != nil {
                    self.lblSymbolSelected.setText("Symbol: " + symbol!)
                } else {
                    //---trying to see if the result can be converted to
                    // NSData---
                    if let emoji = results.first as? NSData {
                        let img = UIImage(data: emoji)
                        //---use the emoji, such as in
                        // an Image control---
                    }
                }
            }
        }
}
```

In this example, you changed the input type to allow an emoji (`WKTextInput-Mode.AllowEmoji`). When the user is done with the input, you try to typecast the first element of the result as a `String`. If this is successful, it means the user has entered (or selected) a text input. It not, you try to typecast the result as `NSData`, because it may contain an emoji. You can then convert the `NSData` to `UIImage` object so that you may display it using an Image control, etc.

2. Because the Apple Watch Simulator does not support emojis, you should run the application on an iPhone with a paired Apple Watch. Once it is running on the watch, tap the **Select Symbol** button (see Figure 3.55). You will be able to select from a list of canned symbols. You can also tap the **Emoji** button to select from a list of emojis.

Figure 3.55 Users can select from a list of emojis

> **Note**
>
> The Apple Watch Simulator does not support emoji inputs.

Laying Out the Controls

So far in this chapter, you have been using the various controls (e.g., Button, Table, Label) to display different types of information—text, images, etc. However, if you drag and drop the controls onto the Interface Controller, you will realize that most of the controls are displayed in a linear top-to-bottom layout. In this section, you will learn how to group controls together using the Group control. The Group control is useful for acting as a container for other controls, and it can align the controls either vertically or horizontally. You can also nest Group controls.

1. Using Xcode, create a new Single View Application project and name it **Layouts**.

2. Add a WatchKit App target to the project. Uncheck the option Include Notification Scene so that we can keep the WatchKit project to a bare minimum.

3. Select the Interface.storyboard file to edit it in the Storyboard Editor.

4. Add a Button control to the Interface Controller (see Figure 3.56).

5. Change the title of the Button to **1** and change its Width and Height to **40** (see Figure 3.57).

Figure 3.56   Adding a Button control to the Interface Controller

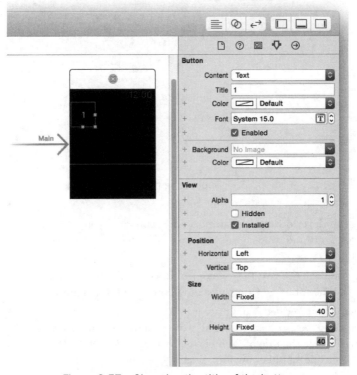

Figure 3.57   Changing the title of the button

6. Copy and paste the Button you modified in the previous step into the Interface Controller (see Figure 3.58) and change its title to **2**. Notice that the next Button is displayed on the next line.

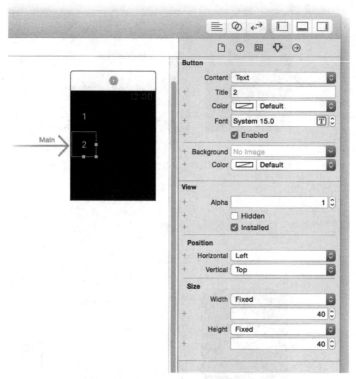

Figure 3.58   Duplicating the Button control

7. To group the two Button controls on the same line, you need to use a Group control. Drag and drop a Group control onto the Interface Controller as shown in Figure 3.59.

8. Drag and drop the two Button controls into the Group control one by one. The layout of the Interface Controller should now look like Figure 3.60.

9. Copy the button titled **2** and paste it into the Group control. Change its title to **3**. Then, copy the Group control and paste it onto the Interface Controller three times. Change the title of each button to **4, 5, 6, 7, 8, 9, ★, 0**, and **#**. The Interface Controller should now look like Figure 3.61.

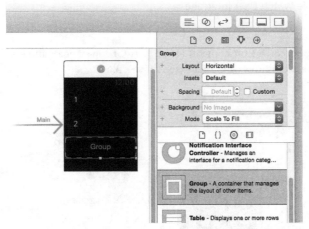

Figure 3.59   Adding a Group control to the Interface Controller

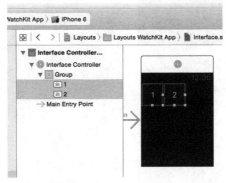

Figure 3.60   Moving the two Button controls into the Group control

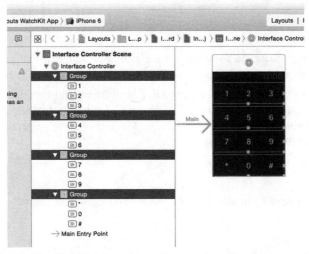

Figure 3.61   The Interface Controller now has four Group controls

10. Select the three Button controls in the first Group control and set their Horizontal position attributes to **Center** (see Figure 3.62).

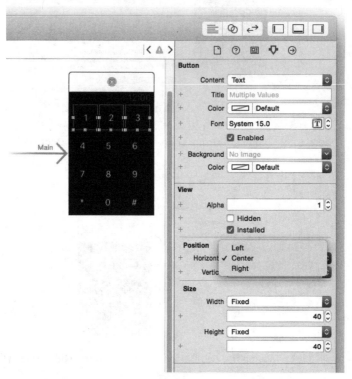

Figure 3.62   Centralizing the three Button controls

11. Repeat the previous step for the buttons in the next three Group controls.

12. Run the application on the iPhone Simulator. The Apple Watch Simulator should now display a nice number pad (see Figure 3.63).

For cases like this, it might be very efficient to have a single action connected to the 12 Button controls. However, in WatchKit, unlike in UIKit (on the iPhone and iPad), the IBAction of each Button does not contain a reference to the Button control initiating the touch:

```
@IBAction func btnClicked() {
}
```

Hence, you have to implement 12 different actions for the 12 buttons.

Figure 3.63   The number pad containing 12 Button controls

Force Touch

One of the unique features of the Apple Watch is Force Touch. Instead of tapping the various controls on the screen, you can press the screen with a small amount of force to bring up the context menu of the current Interface Controller.

Displaying a Context Menu

In this section, you learn how to use Force Touch to display a context menu for your Interface Controller.

1. Using Xcode, create a new Single View Application project and name it **ForceTouch**.

2. Add a WatchKit App target to the project. Uncheck the option Include Notification Scene so that we can keep the WatchKit project to a bare minimum.

3. Select the Interface.storyboard file to edit it in the Storyboard Editor.

4. Add a Menu control to the Interface Controller (see Figure 3.64). Notice that the Menu control is not visible on the Interface Controller, and you can only see it in the hierarchical view.

5. Observe that the Menu control contains another control—Menu Item. Drag and drop another Menu Item control onto the Menu item as shown in Figure 3.65. The Menu control displays a context menu containing up to four menu items.

6. Drag and drop an image named Picture.png onto the Images.xcassets file in the WatchKit App target so that the Menu Item control can display an image (see Figure 3.66). Note that because this is a template image, it is not visible in the Images.xcassets file.

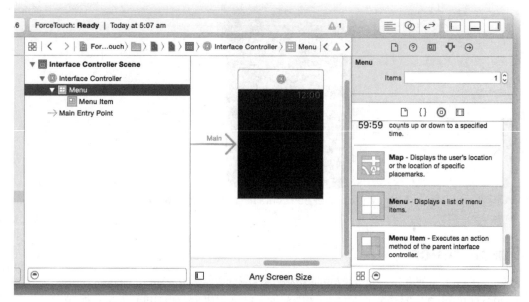

Figure 3.64   Adding a Menu control to the Interface Controller

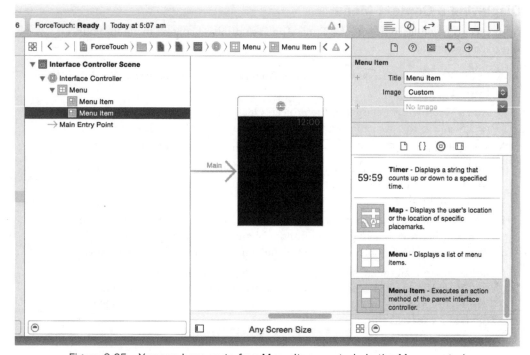

Figure 3.65   You can have up to four Menu Item controls in the Menu control

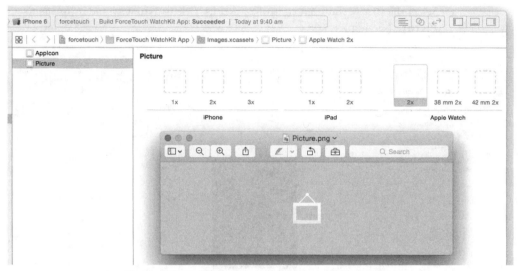

Figure 3.66   Adding a template image to the project

Note

The image to be displayed by the Menu Item control must be a template image. You can find a copy of this image in the source code download for this book.

7. Select the first Menu Item control and set its Title to **Singapore** and its image to **Picture** (see Figure 3.67).

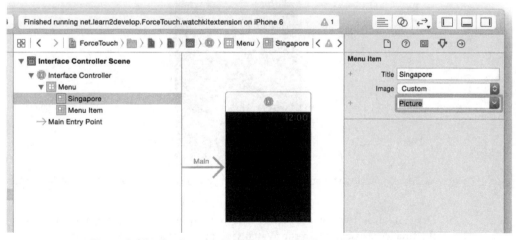

Figure 3.67   Setting the attributes for the first Menu Item control

8. Select the first Menu Item control and set its Title to **Norway** and its image to **Picture** (see Figure 3.68).

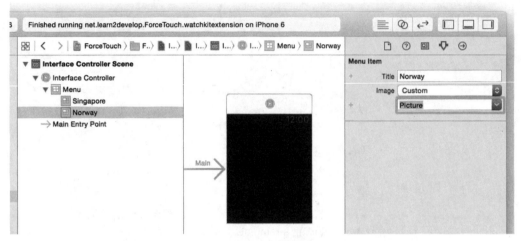

Figure 3.68   Setting the attributes for the second Menu Item control

9. Run the application on the iPhone Simulator. Long-click the Apple Watch Simulator (to simulate Force Touch) and you see the context menu displayed as shown in Figure 3.69. You can click either button to dismiss the context menu.

Figure 3.69   Displaying the context menu when you long-click the Apple Watch Simulator

10. Drag and drop two images named flag_norway.png and flag_singapore.png onto the Images.xcassets file in the WatchKit App target as shown in Figure 3.70.

Note

You can find these two images in the source code download for this book.

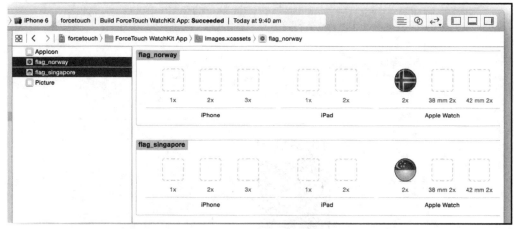

Figure 3.70   Adding the two images to the project

11. Drag and drop an Image control onto the Interface Controller and set its attributes (see Figure 3.71) as follows:

   - Image: **flag_singapore**
   - Horizontal: **Center**
   - Vertical: **Center**

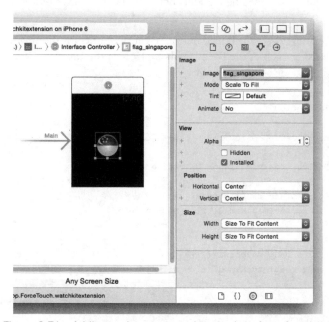

Figure 3.71   Adding an Image control to the Interface Controller

12. Drag and drop a Label control onto the Interface Controller and set Text attributes as shown in Figure 3.72.

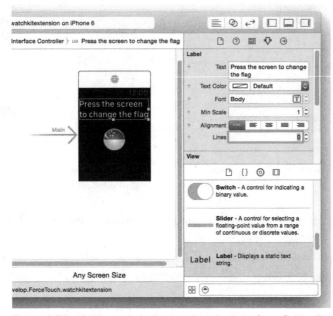

Figure 3.72   Adding a Label control to the Interface Controller

13. Using the Show Assistant Editor button, create an outlet for the Image control and two actions for each of the Menu Item controls in the InterfaceController.swift file. Add the code shown in bold:

```
import WatchKit
import Foundation

class InterfaceController: WKInterfaceController {

    @IBOutlet weak var image: WKInterfaceImage!

    @IBAction func mnuSingapore() {
        image.setImageNamed("flag_singapore")
    }

    @IBAction func mnuNorway() {
        image.setImageNamed("flag_norway")
    }
```

14. Run the application on the iPhone Simulator. Long-click the Apple Watch Simulator and you see the context menu. Selecting either button sets the Image control to display the flag for the respective country (see Figure 3.73).

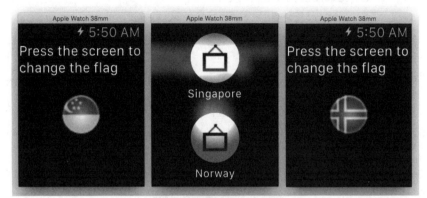

Figure 3.73   Changing the flag by selecting the country in the context menu

Adding Menu Items Programmatically

Instead of adding Menu Item controls to a Menu control during design time, sometimes a situation dictates that you add the Menu Items controls programmatically during runtime.

1. Using the same project used in the previous section, add the following statements in bold to the InterfaceController.swift file:

```swift
import WatchKit
import Foundation

class InterfaceController: WKInterfaceController {

    @IBOutlet weak var image: WKInterfaceImage!

    @IBAction func mnuSingapore() {
        image.setImageNamed("flag_singapore")
    }

    @IBAction func mnuNorway() {
        image.setImageNamed("flag_norway")
    }

    func mnuCancel() {
        //---user tapped Cancel---
    }
```

```
override func awakeWithContext(context: AnyObject?) {
    super.awakeWithContext(context)

    // Configure interface objects here.
    self.addMenuItemWithItemIcon(
        WKMenuItemIcon.Decline,
        title: "Cancel",
        action: "mnuCancel")
}
```

The above statements programmatically add a Menu Item control to the Interface Controller and set its image using one of the built-in icons—Decline. It also sets its title to **Cancel** and assigns its action to the mnuCancel function.

2. Run the application on the iPhone Simulator. When you long-click the Apple Watch Simulator, you will see the context menu as shown in Figure 3.74.

Figure 3.74   The context menu with the third button

3. If you want to set the image to your own, use the addMenuItemWithImageNamed: title:action: method.

Summary

In this chapter, you looked at the various controls that you can use to build the UI of your Apple Watch application. You also looked at how to use Force Touch to display a context Menu in your application. In the next chapter, you look at additional controls, such as Date and Map, as well as how to interact with the containing iOS application to develop really cool Apple Watch applications!

4

Interfacing with iOS Apps

Be a yardstick of quality. Some people aren't used to an environment
where excellence is expected.
Steve Jobs

In the previous chapter, you learned about the various controls that make up the user interface (UI) of an Apple Watch application. Many of the interactions occur between the storyboard and the code in the extension of the project. However, in real-world applications, your code in the extension could not do much (such as accessing web services or getting location information). This is because the extension only runs when the Apple Watch application is running in the foreground of the Apple Watch. A lot of times, the user's interaction with your watch application is brief, and when the user stops interacting with the Apple Watch or exits your application, the Interface Controller is deactivated and the extension is suspended. Hence, you cannot rely on the extension to perform long-running tasks like accessing a web service or obtaining location information. A more reliable way is to let the containing iOS app handle these tasks; the containing iOS app can be configured to execute background tasks for the Apple Watch.

In this chapter, you learn how to write your Apple Watch applications so that you can leverage on the containing iOS application to do much more. You learn how to

- Localize your watch application to support multiple languages
- Communicate between your watch application and the containing iOS app
- Obtain location information
- Access web services
- Share data between the watch application and the containing iOS app
- Expose data using the WatchKit Settings

Localization

Localization is an important topic when it comes to developing applications for the international market. Although you may currently design to display English, you never know when you may need to localize your app for different languages and cultures.

Fortunately, localizing an Apple Watch app is similar to localizing an iOS app. In this section, you learn how to make your watch app display in more than one language:

1. Using Xcode, create a new Single View Application project and name it **Localization**.

2. Add a WatchKit App target to the project. Uncheck the option Include Notification Scene so that we can keep the WatchKit project to a bare minimum.

3. Select the Interface.storyboard file to edit it in the Storyboard Editor.

4. Drag and drop a Label and a Button control onto the storyboard, as shown in Figure 4.1. Set the titles of the controls as shown.

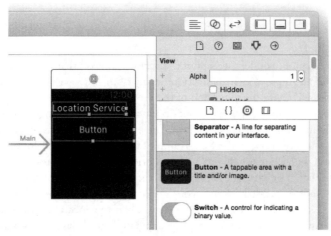

Figure 4.1   Populating the Interface Control with the Label and Button controls

5. Create an outlet and an action for the Button control. This creates the following statements in bold in the InterfaceController.swift file:

```
import WatchKit
import Foundation

class InterfaceController: WKInterfaceController {

    @IBOutlet weak var button: WKInterfaceButton!

    @IBAction func btnClicked() {
    }

    override func awakeWithContext(context: AnyObject?) {
        super.awakeWithContext(context)

        // Configure interface objects here.
    }
```

6. Add the following statements in bold to the InterfaceController.swift file:

```swift
import WatchKit
import Foundation

class InterfaceController: WKInterfaceController {
    var recording = false

    @IBOutlet weak var button: WKInterfaceButton!

    @IBAction func btnClicked() {
        recording = !recording
        if recording {
            button.setTitle("Stop recording")
        } else {
            button.setTitle("Start recording")
        }
    }

    override func awakeWithContext(context: AnyObject?) {
        super.awakeWithContext(context)

        // Configure interface objects here.
        button.setTitle("Start recording")
    }
```

7. Run the application on the iPhone 6 Simulator. Clicking the button toggles its title (see Figure 4.2).

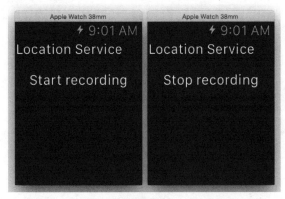

Figure 4.2   Clicking the Button toggles its title

Localizing the User Interface

The application you built in the previous section is hardcoded to display English. If the user changes the language on the iPhone to some other language (such as Chinese or French), the titles on the Label and Button remain in English. A much better user experience is to display the UI of the watch application using the language that the user sets on his iPhone:

1. Select the project name in Xcode and select the **Localization** project on the right (see Figure 4.3). Under the Localizations section, click the **+** button and select the language to which you want to localize. For this example, select **Chinese (Simplified) (zh-Hans)**.

   > **Note**
   >
   > If you want to test this lab exercise using a language that you are familiar with, select the language that you want to localize to, such as Spanish or Norwegian.

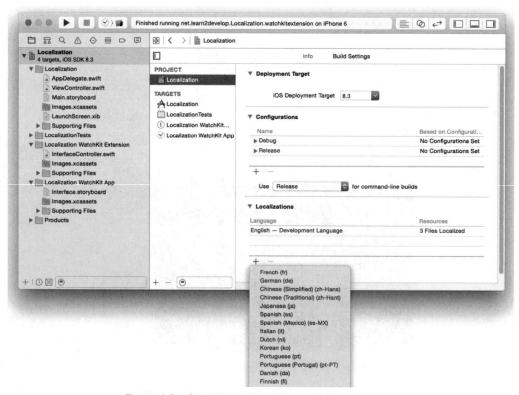

Figure 4.3   Selecting a language to which to localize

2. You are asked which files you want to localize (see Figure 4.4). Accept the defaults selected and click **Finish**. In this case, you are localizing the Main.storyboard (iPhone app), LaunchScreen.xib (iPhone app), and Interface.storyboard (Apple Watch app).

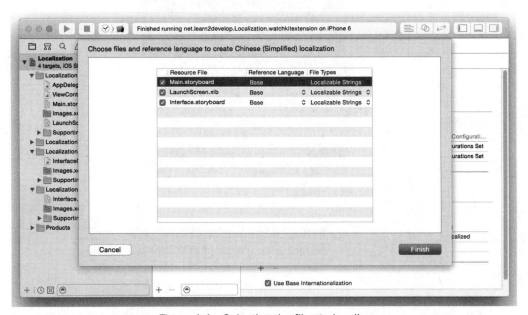

Figure 4.4   Selecting the files to localize

3. The files shown in Figure 4.5 are created in the project.

> **Note**
> The filenames of some of the files are dependent on the language that you have chosen.

4. Select the **Interface.strings (Chinese (Simplified))** file located under the WatchKit app group and observe that it contains the titles of the Label and Button controls, represented as key/value pairs (see Figure 4.6). The system uses this file to load the titles of the Label and Button controls when the language on the iPhone is set to Chinese (Simplified).

5. Change the content of the file, as shown in bold (do not worry about the names such as fA0-eu-oqg or op1-1R-Fn2 as they are generated by Xcode internally):

```
/* Class = "WKInterfaceButton"; title = "Button"; ObjectID = "fA0-eu-oqg"; */
"fA0-eu-oqg.title" = "Button";

/* Class = "WKInterfaceLabel"; text = "Location Service"; ObjectID = "op1-
1R-Fn2"; */
"op1-1R-Fn2.text" = "位置服务";
```

Figure 4.5   The files added to the project after localization

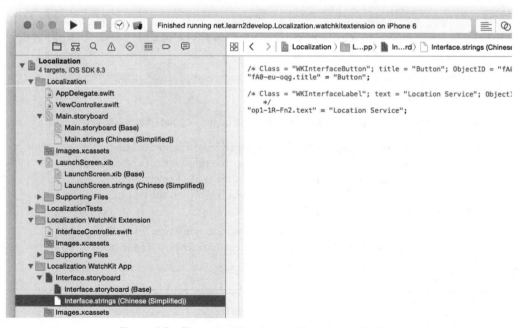

Figure 4.6   The string literals used in your application

Note

If you selected a language other than Chinese in Step 1, you can substitute the Chinese text with the equivalent of **Location Service** in the language that you have selected. For example, **Servicio De Localización** in Spanish, **Beliggenhet service** in Norwegian, etc. Then, in Step 6, simply select the country based on the language you selected.

6. On the iPhone Simulator Home screen, select: **Settings | General | Language & Region | iPhone Language| Chinese, Simplified** (see Figure 4.7)

Figure 4.7   Changing the language on the iPhone

7. Click **Done**.

8. Click **Change to Chinese**, **Simplified**, and the iPhone Simulator reboots.

9. In Xcode, run the application on the iPhone 6 Simulator again, and observe that the Label control on the Apple Watch application now displays its title in Chinese (see Figure 4.8).

Figure 4.8   The title on the Label changes to Chinese (Simplified)

> **Note**
>
> The Button control is still displaying its title in English because the code in the extension programmatically sets its title in English. The next section shows you how to localize the string literals in your application.

Creating Localizable Strings

In the previous section, only the Label control is localized—the Button control does not change. This is because we are setting the title of the Button control programmatically:

```
button.setTitle("Start recording")
```

So how do you localize this string? One way would be to programmatically detect the language set by the user and then set the title accordingly:

```
let lang: String = NSLocale.preferredLanguages()[0] as! String
if lang == "en" {
    button.setTitle("Start recording")
} else {
    button.setTitle("开始录制")
}
```

However, this method is unwieldy and makes your code messy very quickly. A better way would be to create localizable strings so that the system can automatically retrieve the correct string based on the selected language:

1. Using the same project created in the previous section, right-click the extension project and select **New File...**. Select **Resource** under the iOS category and select the **Strings File** template (see Figure 4.9).

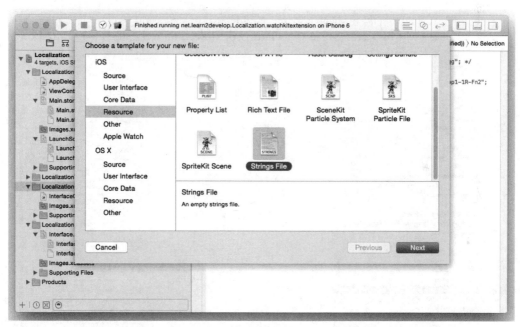

Figure 4.9   Adding a Strings File to the project

2. Name the file **Localizable** (see Figure 4.10) and click **Create**.

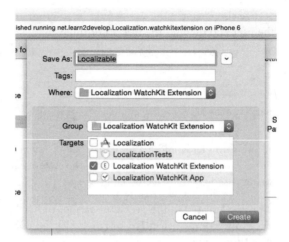

Figure 4.10   Naming the file Localizable

3. A file named Localizable.strings is added to the extension project. Select it and in the File Inspector window, click the **Localize…** button under the Localization section (see Figure 4.11).

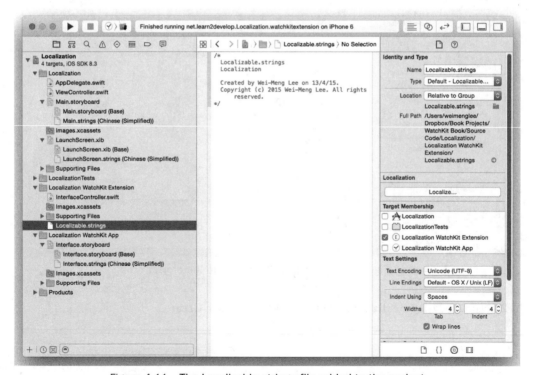

Figure 4.11   The Localizable.strings file added to the project

4. You are asked whether you want to localize the file (see Figure 4.12). Click **Localize**.

Figure 4.12   Select a language to localize

5. In the File Inspector window, you can now see that the Base checkbox is checked (under the Localization section; see Figure 4.13). Now check the **Chinese (Simplified)** checkbox.

Figure 4.13   Selecting additional languages to which to localize

6. You should now see two Localizable.strings files, as shown in Figure 4.14.

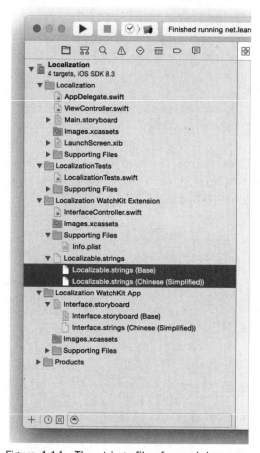

Figure 4.14   The strings files for each language

7. In the Localizable.strings (Base) file, add the following statements:

```
"ButtonTitleStart" = "Start Recording";
"ButtonTitleStop" = "Stop Recording";
```

8. In the Localizable.strings (Chinese (Simplified)) file, add the following statements:

```
"ButtonTitleStart" = "开始录制";
"ButtonTitleStop" = "停止录制";
```

9. Add the following statements in bold to the InterfaceController.swift file:

```
import WatchKit
import Foundation
```

```swift
class InterfaceController: WKInterfaceController {

    var recording = false

    @IBOutlet weak var button: WKInterfaceButton!

    @IBAction func btnClicked() {
        recording = !recording
        /*
        if recording {
            button.setTitle("Stop recording")
        } else {
            button.setTitle("Start recording")
        }
        */
        let buttonTitle: String
        if recording {
            buttonTitle = NSLocalizedString("ButtonTitleStop",
                comment: "Localized Title for Stop Recording button")

        } else {
            buttonTitle = NSLocalizedString("ButtonTitleStart",
                comment: "Localized Title for Start Recording button")
        }
        button.setTitle(buttonTitle)
    }
}
```

The `NSLocalizedString:comment:` method returns a localized string, based on the key (`ButtonTitleStop` or `ButtonTitleStart`) that you have defined in the Localizable.strings files.

10. Run the application on the iPhone Simulator. You should now see the Button displayed in Chinese (see Figure 4.15).

Figure 4.15   The Button control now displays the title in Chinese (Simplified)

11. If you set the iPhone Simulator back to English and rerun the application, the Label and Button controls on the Apple Watch Simulator will display in English.

> **Note**
>
> If you want to change the language for the iPhone Simulator back to English (now that it is in Chinese), the simplest way is to go to the iOS Simulator menu and select **Reset Content and Settings….** Then, select **Reset**. This will reset the iPhone Simulator back to English.

Using the Date Control

Besides the various controls that you have seen in the previous chapter, there is one more control that we have not discussed: Date. The Date control displays the current date and time, and you can customize it to display in whatever format you prefer. Best of all, it automatically localizes based on the language selected by the user:

1. Using the same project you have used in the previous section, add a Date control to the Interface Controller (see Figure 4.16).

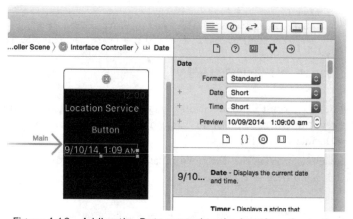

Figure 4.16   Adding the Date control to the Interface Controller

2. Observe that, in the Attributes Inspector window, you can change the Format of the Date control to Custom and then specify the format to display the date and time (see Figure 4.17).

3. Run the application on the iPhone Simulator and observe the date and time displayed when the language on the iPhone is set to English, Chinese (Simplified), and Japanese, respectively (see Figure 4.18).

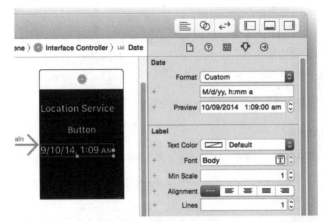

Figure 4.17   You can customize the display of the Date control

Figure 4.18   The Date control displayed in different languages

Communicating between the WatchKit App and the Extension

As you learned in Chapter 1, "Getting Started with WatchKit Programming," the WatchKit extension runs only when the WatchKit app is running, and it does not support background execution. Hence, for tasks that might take time to complete, it is advisable to send the request to the containing iOS to perform the tasks, which can be configured to run in the background.

There are a few scenarios where this is necessary:

- Your application needs to get the location of the user.
- Your application needs to consume a web service (such as to fetch weather or stock prices).

In the following sections, you learn how to do these things.

Location Data

Let's start by creating an Apple Watch application that reports your current location:

1. Using Xcode, create a new Single View Application project and name it **GetLocation**.

2. Add a WatchKit App target to the project. Uncheck the option Include Notification Scene so that we can keep the WatchKit project to a bare minimum.

3. Select the Interface.storyboard file to edit it in the Storyboard Editor.

4. Drag and drop a Button and a Label control onto the storyboard, as shown in Figure 4.19. For the Label control, set the Lines attribute to 0.

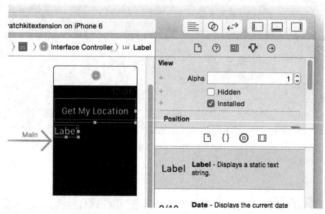

Figure 4.19   Populating the Interface Controller with the Button and Label controls

5. Create an outlet for the Label control and an action for the Button. This adds the statements in bold in the InterfaceController.swift file:

```
import WatchKit
import Foundation

class InterfaceController: WKInterfaceController {
```

```
@IBOutlet weak var label: WKInterfaceLabel!

@IBAction func btnGetMyLocation() {
}

override func awakeWithContext(context: AnyObject?) {
    super.awakeWithContext(context)

    // Configure interface objects here.
}
```

6. Add the following statements in bold to the InterfaceController.swift file:

```
import WatchKit
import Foundation

class InterfaceController: WKInterfaceController {

    @IBOutlet weak var label: WKInterfaceLabel!

    @IBAction func btnGetMyLocation() {
        WKInterfaceController.openParentApplication([:]) {
            (replyDataFromPhone, error) -> Void in


        }
    }
```

The previous code calls the openParentApplication: method to invoke the containing iOS application. You can pass data to the iOS application through the first parameter of this method. In this example, you pass an empty dictionary ([:]) to the containing iOS app. When the iOS app returns, it calls the reply block of the openParentApplication: method, with the result encapsulated in the first argument (replyDataFromPhone) and any errors in the second argument (error). For this example, you would want the iOS app to find your current location and return it to the extension project. You will add the code later in this section to receive the data returned by the iOS app.

7. Select the project name in Xcode and click the **Build Phases** tab (ensure that the **GetLocation** target is selected; see Figure 4.20). Expand the Link Binary With Libraries section and click the **+** button.

8. Select **CoreLocation.framework** and click **Add** (see Figure 4.21).

9. Add a new Swift file to the iOS project (see Figure 4.22) and name it **GetCurrentLocation.swift**.

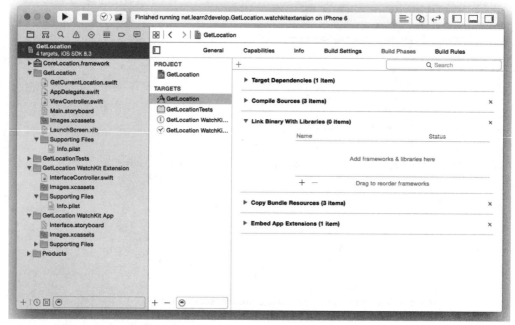

Figure 4.20   Preparing to add a new framework to the project

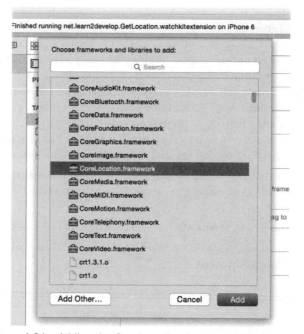

Figure 4.21   Adding the CoreLocation framework to the project

Figure 4.22   Adding a new Swift file to the project

10. Populate the GetCurrentLocation.swift file as follows:

```swift
import Foundation
import CoreLocation

class GetCurrentLocation:NSObject, CLLocationManagerDelegate {
    var lm: CLLocationManager!

    //---the closure that is fired containing the location obtained
    // and error (if any)---
    typealias LocationObtainedClosure = (
        (location: CLLocation?, error: NSError?)->()
    )
    var didCompleteHandler: LocationObtainedClosure!

    //---when a location has been found---
    func locationManager(manager: CLLocationManager!,
        didUpdateLocations locations: [AnyObject]!) {

        //---stop finding location---
        lm.stopUpdatingLocation()

        //---get the most recent location---
        var currentLocation = locations.last as! CLLocation

        //---inform the caller and pass it the location---
        didCompleteHandler(location: currentLocation, error: nil)

        //---set the lm and delegate to nil---
        lm.delegate = nil
        lm = nil
    }
```

```
//---failed to find a location---
func locationManager(manager: CLLocationManager!,
    didFailWithError error: NSError!) {

    //---report the error to the caller---
    didCompleteHandler(location: nil, error: error)
}

//---caller will call this function and implement the
// closure to get the single location---
func getLocationWithCompletion(completion: LocationObtainedClosure) {
    didCompleteHandler = completion

    lm = CLLocationManager()
    lm.delegate = self
    lm.desiredAccuracy = 0
    lm.distanceFilter = 0
    lm.startUpdatingLocation()
}
}
```

The motives of creating the `GetCurrentLocation` class are

- To use the `CLLocationManager` to get the current location
- To provide a method to let users of this class obtain the single current location without worrying about implementing the delegates for the `CLLocationManager`
- To return the location obtained via a closure
- To allow the `CLLocationManager`, once the location is obtained, to stop monitoring for location changes

11. Add the following statements in bold to the AppDelegate.swift file:

```
import UIKit
import CoreLocation

@UIApplicationMain
class AppDelegate: UIResponder, UIApplicationDelegate {

    var window: UIWindow?

    var manager: GetCurrentLocation!
    var backgroundTaskIdentifier:UIBackgroundTaskIdentifier!

    func application(application: UIApplication,
        handleWatchKitExtensionRequest userInfo: [NSObject : AnyObject]?,
        reply: (([NSObject : AnyObject]!) -> Void)!) {
```

```
    backgroundTaskIdentifier =
        application.beginBackgroundTaskWithName("GetMyLocation",
            expirationHandler: { () -> Void in
            //---this handler is fired after 10 minutes---
            // task is suspended to do some housekeeping
            if self.backgroundTaskIdentifier !=
                UIBackgroundTaskInvalid {
                application.endBackgroundTask(
                    self.backgroundTaskIdentifier)
                self.backgroundTaskIdentifier =
                    UIBackgroundTaskInvalid
            }
    })

    //---get the current single location---
    manager = GetCurrentLocation()

    manager.getLocationWithCompletion {
        (location, error) -> () in
        if location != nil {
            var lat = "\(location!.coordinate.latitude)"
            var lng =
                "\(location!.coordinate.longitude)"
            var dataToWatch = [
                "lat" : lat,
                "lng" : lng
            ]
            reply(dataToWatch)
        } else {
            reply(nil)
        }
    }
    //---background task is done---
    application.endBackgroundTask(backgroundTaskIdentifier)
    backgroundTaskIdentifier = UIBackgroundTaskInvalid

}

func application(application: UIApplication,
    didFinishLaunchingWithOptions launchOptions:
    [NSObject: AnyObject]?) -> Bool {
    // Override point for customization after application launch.

    return true
}
```

In the previous code:

- You implement the `application:handleWatchKitExtensionRequest: reply:` method. This method is called whenever the extension calls the `openParentApplication:` method.

- The data passed from the watch is obtained through the `userInfo` argument. For this example, the watch is passing an empty dictionary to the iOS app.

- Because the `application:handleWatchKitExtensionRequest:reply:` method is called while the iOS app is in the background, you should call the `beginBackgroundTaskWithName:expirationHandler:` method to ensure that your app is not suspended before it has a chance to send a reply back to the extension project.

- You create an instance of the `GetCurrentLocation` class and call its `getLocationWithCompletion:` method to obtain the user's current location.

- The location obtained by the `GetCurrentLocation` class is returned as a closure. It is essential that you use this technique to get the current location as you need to return the location within the `application:handleWatch- KitExtensionRequest:reply:` method.

- You create a dictionary named `dataToWatch` to return the latitude and longitude via the `lat` and `lng` keys.

12. In the Info.plist file for the iOS app, add a new key named **NSLocationAlways- UsageDescription**, and set it to a value of **Obtain your location when the app is in the background** (see Figure 4.23).

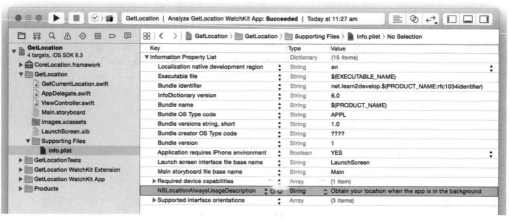

Figure 4.23   Adding a new key to the Info.plist file

13. Add the following statements in bold to the ViewController.swift file:

```
import UIKit
import CoreLocation

class ViewController: UIViewController {

    var lm: CLLocationManager!

    override func viewDidLoad() {
        super.viewDidLoad()
        // Do any additional setup after loading the view, typically from a nib.

        //---request for background location use---
        lm = CLLocationManager()
        lm.requestAlwaysAuthorization()
    }

    override func didReceiveMemoryWarning() {
        super.didReceiveMemoryWarning()
        // Dispose of any resources that can be recreated.
    }
}
```

You need to request permission to let the application obtain the user's location in the background. If not, the application will not be able to obtain the location through the CLLocationManager. This should be done when the user runs the iOS application for the first time after it has been installed.

14. Back in the InterfaceController.swift file, add in the following statements in bold:

```
@IBAction func btnGetMyLocation() {
    WKInterfaceController.openParentApplication([:]) {
        (replyDataFromPhone, error) -> Void in

        if replyDataFromPhone != nil {
            var location = replyDataFromPhone as NSDictionary
            var lat = location["lat"] as? String
            var lng = location["lng"] as? String
            var s = "Location is: \(lat!),\(lng!)"
            self.label.setText(s)
        } else {
            self.label.setText("Can't get location")
        }
    }
}

override func awakeWithContext(context: AnyObject?) {
    super.awakeWithContext(context)
```

```
    // Configure interface objects here.
    label.setText("")
}
```

In this case, when the iOS app returns the location through the `replyData-FromPhone` argument, you extract the value of the `lat` and `lng` keys and then display the information on the Label control.

15. To test the application, you first need to run the iOS application on the iPhone Simulator. Select the **GetLocation** scheme (see Figure 4.24) and then run it on the iPhone Simulator.

Figure 4.24   Selecting the GetLocation scheme

16. On the iPhone Simulator, you are asked to give permission to allow the app to access your location even if you are not using the app. Click **Allow** (see Figure 4.25).

Figure 4.25   Obtaining permission from the user to access
location when the application is in the background

17. Select the **GetLocation WatchKit App** scheme (see Figure 4.26) on Xcode and run the application.

Figure 4.26   Changing to the WatchKit App scheme

18. On the iPhone Simulator, select the **Debug | Location | Freeway Drive** menu item so that simulated locations can be sent to the iPhone Simulator. On the Apple Watch Simulator, click the **Get My Location** button and, after a while, you should see the location, as shown in Figure 4.27.

Figure 4.27   Displaying the location on the Apple Watch

Displaying Maps

Displaying the location information in latitude and longitude is not useful to the user. A better way would be to display a map so that the user can visually know where he is. In WatchKit, you can use the Map control to display a static map.

> **Note**
>
> At this moment, the WatchKit does not support dynamic maps. So, you won't be able to display a map that you can pan in real time.

1. Add a Map control onto the Interface Controller in the Interface.storyboard file (see Figure 4.28).

Figure 4.28   Adding the Map control to the Interface Controller

2. Create an outlet for the Map control, and this creates the following bold statement in the InterfaceController.swift file:

```
import WatchKit
import Foundation


class InterfaceController: WKInterfaceController {

    @IBOutlet weak var label: WKInterfaceLabel!
    @IBOutlet weak var map: WKInterfaceMap!
```

3. Add the following statements in bold to the InterfaceController.swift file:

```
@IBAction func btnGetMyLocation() {
    WKInterfaceController.openParentApplication([:]) {
        (replyDataFromPhone, error) -> Void in

        if replyDataFromPhone != nil {
            var location = replyDataFromPhone as NSDictionary
            var lat = location["lat"] as? String
            var lng = location["lng"] as? String
            var s = "Location is: \(lat!),\(lng!)"
```

```
            // self.label.setText(s)

            let loc = CLLocationCoordinate2D(
                latitude: (lat! as NSString).doubleValue,
                longitude: (lng! as NSString).doubleValue)

            let coordinateSpan =  MKCoordinateSpan(
                latitudeDelta: 0.010, longitudeDelta: 0.010)

            self.map.setHidden(false)
            self.map.addAnnotation(loc, withPinColor: .Purple)
            self.map.setRegion(MKCoordinateRegion(
                center: loc, span: coordinateSpan))
        } else {
            self.label.setText("Can't get location")
        }
    }
}

override func awakeWithContext(context: AnyObject?) {
    super.awakeWithContext(context)

    // Configure interface objects here.
    label.setText("")
    map.setHidden(true)
}
```

4. Run the application on the iPhone Simulator and the Apple Watch Simulator, and click the **Get My Location** button (see Figure 4.29). You should now be able to see the map showing your current location (as reported by the iPhone Simulator).

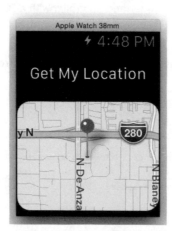

Figure 4.29   The watch application displaying the location using the Map control

Accessing Web Services

Another common scenario is accessing web services. For example, your application might allow the user to tap a button to check on the latest weather information by connecting to a web service:

1. Using Xcode, create a new Single View Application project and name it **WebServices**.
2. Add a WatchKit App target to the project.
3. Select the Interface.storyboard file to edit it in the Storyboard Editor.
4. Drag and drop a Button and a Label control onto the storyboard, as shown in Figure 4.30. Set the Lines attribute of the Label control to 0.

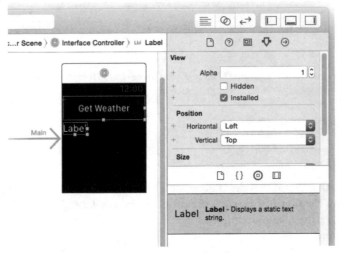

Figure 4.30   Populating the Interface Controller with a Button and a Label control

5. Create an outlet for the Label control and an action for the Button. This creates the following statements in bold in the InterfaceController.swift file:

```
import WatchKit
import Foundation

class InterfaceController: WKInterfaceController {

    @IBOutlet weak var label: WKInterfaceLabel!

    @IBAction func btnGetWeather() {
    }
```

```
override func awakeWithContext(context: AnyObject?) {
    super.awakeWithContext(context)

    // Configure interface objects here.
}
```

6. Add the following statements in bold to the InterfaceController.swift file:

```
import WatchKit
import Foundation

class InterfaceController: WKInterfaceController {

    @IBOutlet weak var label: WKInterfaceLabel!

    @IBAction func btnGetWeather() {
        //---send the country to the iOS app---
        var country = "SINGAPORE"
        let dataToPhone = [
            "country" : country,
        ]

        WKInterfaceController.openParentApplication(dataToPhone) {
            (replyDataFromPhone, error) -> Void in
            if replyDataFromPhone != nil {
                //---extract the temperature from the result returned by the
                // iOS app---
                var temperature = replyDataFromPhone["temp"] as! Double
                var temperatureStr = String(format:"%.2f", temperature)
                self.label.setText("Temperature in " + country +
                    " is \(temperatureStr) Degrees Celsius")
            } else {
                self.label.setText("Error")
            }
        }
    }

    override func awakeWithContext(context: AnyObject?) {
        super.awakeWithContext(context)

        // Configure interface objects here.
        label.setText("")
    }
}
```

In the previous code:

- You create a dictionary named dataToPhone, with one key named country and its value set to SINGAPORE.

- You call the openParentApplication: method to pass the dataToPhone dictionary to the containing iOS app. When the iOS app returns, it calls the reply block of the openParentApplication: method, with the result encapsulated in the first argument (replyDataFromPhone) and any errors in the second argument (error).

- The temperature of a country is returned via the replyDataFromPhone dictionary, via the key named temp. The value is then displayed in the Label control.

7. In the AppDelegate.swift file in the iOS project, add the following statements in bold:

```swift
import UIKit

@UIApplicationMain
class AppDelegate: UIResponder, UIApplicationDelegate {

    var window: UIWindow?
    var taskID: UIBackgroundTaskIdentifier!

    //---parse the json string---
    func parseJSONData(data: NSData) -> Double {
        var error: NSError?
        var parsedJSONData = NSJSONSerialization.JSONObjectWithData(data,
            options: NSJSONReadingOptions.allZeros,
            error: &error) as! NSDictionary

        var main = parsedJSONData["main"] as! NSDictionary

        //---temperature in Kelvin---
        var temp = main["temp"] as! Double

        //---convert temperature to Celsius---
        return temp - 273;
    }

    func application(application: UIApplication,
            handleWatchKitExtensionRequest userInfo: [NSObject : AnyObject]?,
            reply: (([NSObject : AnyObject]!) -> Void)!) {

        //---cast the data from the extension as a dictionary---
        var dataFromPhone = userInfo! as NSDictionary

        //---url of the web service---
        var urlString = "http://api.openweathermap.org/data/2.5/weather?q=" +
            (dataFromPhone["country"] as!
```

```
        String).stringByAddingPercentEncodingWithAllowedCharacters(
        .URLHostAllowedCharacterSet())!
    var session = NSURLSession.sharedSession()

    //---start a background task with expiration---
    taskID = application.beginBackgroundTaskWithName(
        "backgroundTask",
        expirationHandler: { () -> Void in
        if self.taskID != UIBackgroundTaskInvalid {
            application.endBackgroundTask(self.taskID)
            self.taskID = UIBackgroundTaskInvalid
        }
    })

    session.dataTaskWithURL(NSURL(string:urlString)!,
        completionHandler: {
        (data, response, error) -> Void in

        var httpResp = response as! NSHTTPURLResponse
        if error == nil && httpResp.statusCode == 200 {
            var result = NSString(bytes: data.bytes,
                length: data.length, encoding: NSUTF8StringEncoding)

            //---parse the JSON result---
            var temp = self.parseJSONData(data)

            //---send the temp back to the extension---
            var dataToWatch = [
                "temp" : temp
            ]
            reply(dataToWatch)
        } else {
            reply([:])
        }

        //---end the background task---
        application.endBackgroundTask(self.taskID)
        self.taskID = UIBackgroundTaskInvalid
    }).resume()
}
```

In the previous code:

- You implement the `application:handleWatchKitExtensionRequest:` `reply:` method. This method is called whenever the extension calls the `openParentApplication:` method.

- The data passed from the watch is obtained through the userInfo argument. The country to get the weather is extracted from the userInfo dictionary via the country key.

- You use the NSURLSession class to connect to the web service so that you can fetch the weather of the specified country. The web service returns the result in JSON format, and you define a method named parseJSONData: to extract the temperature.

- You create a dictionary named dataToWatch to return the temperature via the temp key.

8. Run the application on the iPhone Simulator. On the Apple Watch Simulator, click the **Get Weather** button and observe the result displayed (see Figure 4.31).

Figure 4.31   Displaying the temperature on the watch application

Sharing Data

So far, you have accomplished quite a bit:

- You are able to pass data from the extension to the containing iOS app.

- You have learned how to consume a web service in the background on the iOS app.

- You are able to pass the data back to the extension.

Despite all these achievements, there is still some work left to do. The country to check for the weather is hardcoded in the extension project. It would be more convenient to allow the user to select from a list of countries in the containing iOS app. For this, you can use the NSUserDefaults class to save data on the iOS app and then access the data from the extension project. The following section shows how to do this.

Creating a Shared App Group

In iOS development, it is common to use the NSUserDefaults class to persist data using key/value pairs. You can continue to use this approach in your Apple Watch application. However, note the following:

- The data that you saved using the NSUserDefaults class in the iOS app is not visible by default to the extension project. The same applies to the data saved in the extension project. The data saved in each app is saved in its private container, and neither app has the rights to access the data in the other container.

- To allow both apps to access the same set of data, you need to create a shared container known as a *shared app group*.

- Data saved to this shared app group is now accessible by the containing iOS app and the extension project.

In the following exercise, you will learn how to create a shared app group so that you can share data between the watch app and the containing iOS app.

1. Using the same project used in the previous section, select the project name in Xcode and select the **WebServices** target (see Figure 4.32). Select the **Capabilities** tab and locate the App Groups section. Turn on the App Groups capability.

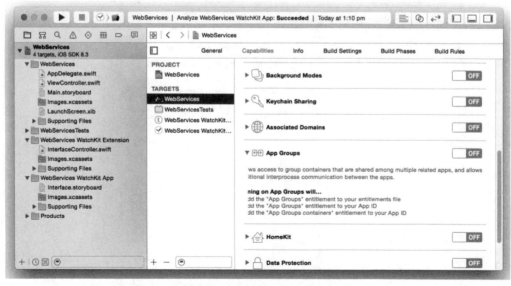

Figure 4.32   Turning on the App Groups feature

2. To enable App Groups, you need to enroll in the Apple Developer Program. Click **Add...** to enter your Apple ID (see Figure 4.33).

Figure 4.33   Adding an Apple ID account

> **Note**
>
> You can enroll in the Apple Developer Program at: https://developer.apple.com/
> programs/ios/. The program costs $99/year.

3. Enter your Apple ID and Password (see Figure 4.34) and then click **Add**.

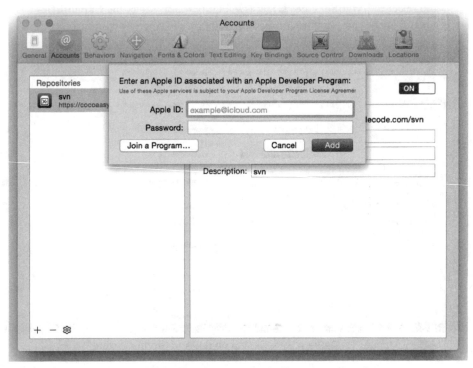

Figure 4.34   Entering your Apple ID and password

4. Once you have successfully logged in, select the development team to use (see Figure 4.35) and click **Choose**.

Figure 4.35   Selecting a development team to use for provisioning

5. Under the App Groups section, you may see some existing app groups already created (if you have added them in some other projects). Click the **+** button to add a new app group (see Figure 4.36).

Figure 4.36   Adding a new app group

6. The container name starts with "group.". For this example, give it a unique name, like: group.learningwatchkit.webservices.app (see Figure 4.37).

Figure 4.37   Naming the new container

> **Note**
>
> You have to use a unique name for the new container.

7. The new app group should now appear in the App Groups section (see Figure 4.38).

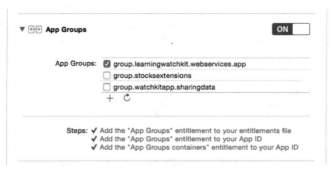

Figure 4.38   Viewing the newly created app group

> **Note**
>
> Click the refresh button if you encountered errors in creating the app group. Also, if you have problems in creating the shared app group, check to ensure that you have a valid provisioning profile installed on your Mac.

8. In the WebServices WatchKit Extension target, likewise turn on the App Groups capability (see Figure 4.39).

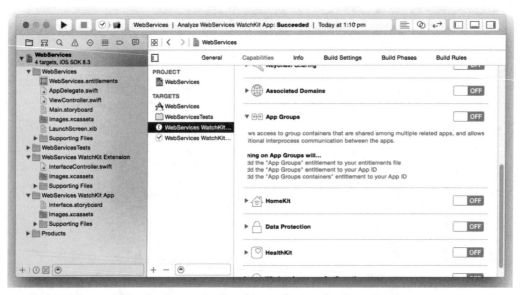

Figure 4.39   Turning on the App Groups feature for the extension target

9. You should see the app group previously created. Check it (see Figure 4.40).

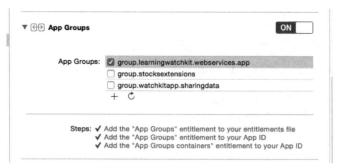

Figure 4.40   The previously created app group should now appear

Saving Data in the Shared Container

With the shared app group created, you can now save data into it:

1. Add the following views to the View window in the Main.storyboard file in the containing iOS app (see Figure 4.41):

   ▪ Label
   ▪ Picker

Figure 4.41   Populating the View Controller

2. Create an outlet for the Picker view, and you should see the following statement in bold in the ViewController.swift file:

```
import UIKit

class ViewController: UIViewController {

    @IBOutlet weak var pickerCountries: UIPickerView!

    override func viewDidLoad() {
        super.viewDidLoad()
        // Do any additional setup after loading the view, typically from a nib.
    }

    override func didReceiveMemoryWarning() {
        super.didReceiveMemoryWarning()
        // Dispose of any resources that can be recreated.
    }

}
```

3. Add the following statements in bold to the ViewController.swift file:

```
import UIKit

class ViewController: UIViewController,
    UIPickerViewDataSource,
    UIPickerViewDelegate {

    @IBOutlet weak var pickerCountries: UIPickerView!

    var countries: [String]!

    override func viewDidLoad() {
        super.viewDidLoad()
        // Do any additional setup after loading the view, typically from a nib.
        countries = ["Singapore", "Norway", "Japan", "Thailand", "Hong Kong"]
        self.pickerCountries.delegate = self
        self.pickerCountries.dataSource = self
    }

    func numberOfComponentsInPickerView(pickerView: UIPickerView) -> Int {
        return 1
    }

    func pickerView(pickerView: UIPickerView,
            numberOfRowsInComponent component: Int) -> Int {
        return countries.count
    }
```

```
func pickerView(pickerView: UIPickerView, titleForRow row: Int,
        forComponent component: Int) -> String! {
    return countries[row]
}


func pickerView(pickerView: UIPickerView, didSelectRow row: Int,
        inComponent component: Int) {

    //---replace "group.learningwatchkit.webservices.app" with the string
    // that you have created earlier---
    var defaults = NSUserDefaults(
        suiteName: "group.learningwatchkit.webservices.app")
    defaults?.setObject(countries[row], forKey: "country")
    defaults?.synchronize()
}

override func didReceiveMemoryWarning() {
    super.didReceiveMemoryWarning()
    // Dispose of any resources that can be recreated.
}
}
```

The previous code populates the Picker view with a list of country names. When the user selects a country, the country is saved using the NSUserDefaults class. The initializer for the NSUserDefaults class takes in the name of the shared app group (group.learningwatchkit.webservices.app) that you have created in the previous section.

> **Note**
>
> Be sure to replace "group.learningwatchkit.webservices.app" with the name that you have used for your project.

4. In Xcode, select the **WebServices** scheme (see Figure 4.42) and run the application on the iPhone Simulator.

Figure 4.42   Selecting the WebServices scheme

5. On the iPhone Simulator, select a country from the Picker view (see Figure 4.43). The country selected is now saved into the shared app group container.

Figure 4.43   Selecting a country on the iPhone Simulator

Retrieving Data from the Shared Container

Now that you have learned how to save data into the shared container in the iOS app, the next thing to do is to retrieve the saved data from the extension project:

1. Add the following statements in bold to the InterfaceController.swift file:

```
import WatchKit
import Foundation

class InterfaceController: WKInterfaceController {

    @IBOutlet weak var label: WKInterfaceLabel!

    @IBAction func btnGetWeather() {
        //---replace "group.learningwatchkit.webservices.app" with the string
        // that you have created earlier---
        var defaults = NSUserDefaults(
            suiteName: "group.learningwatchkit.webservices.app")

        //---send the country to the iOS app---
        var country = defaults?.objectForKey("country") as! String
        let dataToPhone = [
            "country" : country,
        ]
```

```
WKInterfaceController.openParentApplication(dataToPhone) {
    (replyDataFromPhone, error) -> Void in
    if replyDataFromPhone != nil {
        //---extract the temperature from the result returned by the
        // iOS app---
        var temperature = replyDataFromPhone["temp"] as! Double
        var temperatureStr = String(format:"%.2f", temperature)

        self.label.setText("Temperature in " + country +
            " is \(temperatureStr) Degrees Celsius")
    } else {
        self.label.setText("Error")
    }
}
}
```

2. Run the application on the iPhone Simulator. Click the **Get Weather** button (see Figure 4.44), and you see the weather for Japan (based on the country that you selected earlier on the iPhone Simulator).

Figure 4.44   The watch application displaying the weather of
the country selected on the iPhone Simulator

Using the WatchKit Settings

So far, so good! The user is able to select the country in the iOS app, and the corresponding watch application is able to load the weather for the selected country. It would be even better if we could change the country without even loading the iOS application. You could expose the data saved using the `NSUserDefaults` class through the Settings application. In WatchKit, you can expose the data through the special Apple Watch application on your iPhone:

1. Using the same project (WebServices) used in the previous section, right-click the project name (see Figure 4.45) and select **New File…**.

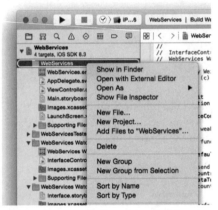

Figure 4.45   Adding a new file to the WebServices project

2. Under the iOS category, select **Apple Watch** and then **WatchKit Settings Bundle** (see Figure 4.46).

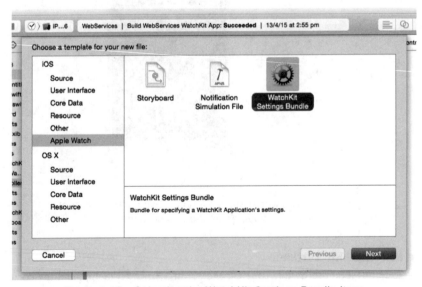

Figure 4.46   Selecting the WatchKit Settings Bundle item

3. Accept the default name of Settings–Watch and click **Create** (see Figure 4.47).

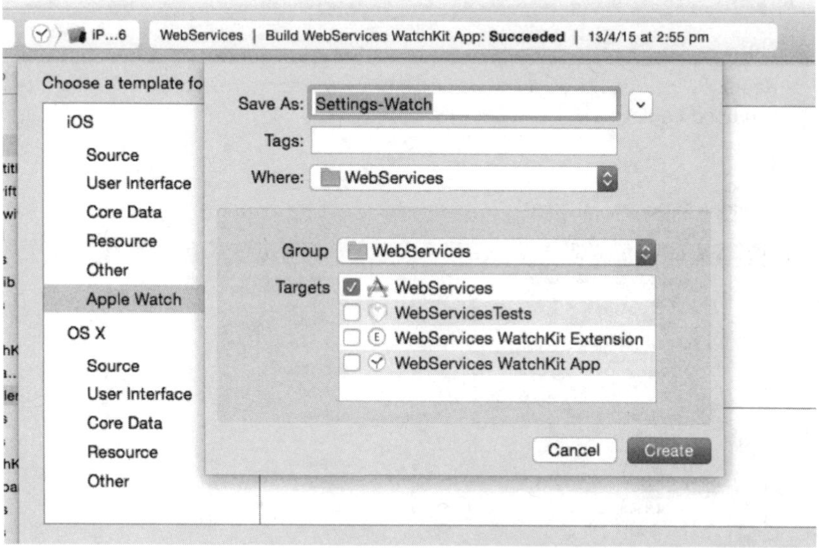

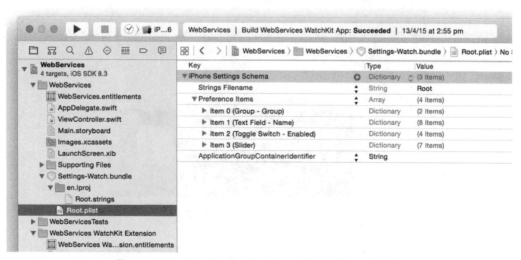

Figure 4.47   Naming the file Settings-Watch

4. A file named Settings–Watch.bundle is now added to the project (see Figure 4.48). Expand it and click the **Root.plist** file. You see four items in it (named Item 0, Item 1, etc.). Delete the four items.

Figure 4.48   Viewing the four items in the Root.plist file

5. Add the items as shown in Figure 4.49 to the Root.plist file. Also, set the value of the ApplicationGroupContainerIdentifier key to "`group.learningwatchkit .webservices.app`".

> **Note**
>
> Replace "`group.learningwatchkit.webservices.app`" with the string that you used earlier.

Key	Type	Value
▼ iPhone Settings Schema	Dictionary	(3 items)
Strings Filename	String	Root
Preference Items	Array	(2 items)
▼ Item 0 (Group - Weather for	Dictionary	(2 items)
Type	String	Group
Title	String	Weather for country
▼ Item 1 (Multi Value - Country)	Dictionary	(5 items)
Type	String	Multi Value
Title	String	Country
Identifier	String	country
▼ Titles	Array	(5 items)
Item 0	String	Singapore
Item 1	String	Norway
Item 2	String	Japan
Item 3	String	Thailand
Item 4	String	Hong Kong
▼ Values	Array	(5 items)
Item 0	String	Singapore
Item 1	String	Norway
Item 2	String	Japan
Item 3	String	Thailand
Item 4	String	Hong Kong
ApplicationGroupContainerIdentifier	String	group.learningwatchkit.webservices.app

Figure 4.49   Adding the new items to the Root.plist file

6. Run the application on the iPhone Simulator. On the iPhone Simulator, locate the Apple Watch application (see Figure 4.50), and click it to launch it.

Figure 4.50   Locating the Apple Watch application on the iPhone Simulator

7. You should be able to see the WebServices app listed in the WatchKitSettings page (see left of Figure 4.51). Click the **WebServices** item and you should see

the country currently selected (see middle of Figure 4.51). Click it and you will be able to select other countries (see right of Figure 4.51).

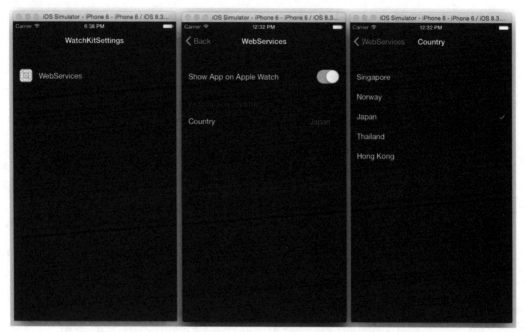

Figure 4.51   Accessing the settings for the WebServices application

8. If you select another country—Norway, for example—clicking the **Get Weather** button in your watch application fetches the weather for Norway.

Sharing Files

Up until this point, all the data we have shared is in the form of NSUserDefaults key/value pairs. However, often we may also need to share files between the watch app and the containing iOS app. In the following exercise, you will see how this can be done. Specifically, after the user has selected a country in the iOS app, the application will proceed to download the flag for the selected country. The flag that is downloaded will then be displayed on the watch application.

1. Using the same project (WebServices) used in the previous section, add the following statements in bold to the ViewController.swift file located in the iOS app:

```
import UIKit

class ViewController: UIViewController,
    UIPickerViewDataSource,
    UIPickerViewDelegate {
```

```swift
@IBOutlet weak var pickerCountries: UIPickerView!

var countries: [String]!

//---download image from the Web---
func downloadImage(urlString:String) {
    var imgURL = NSURL(string: urlString)
    var request: NSURLRequest = NSURLRequest(URL: imgURL!)
    var urlConnection = NSURLConnection(request: request, delegate: self)

    NSURLConnection.sendAsynchronousRequest(request,
        queue: NSOperationQueue.mainQueue(),
        completionHandler: {
            (response: NSURLResponse!,
             data: NSData!,
             error: NSError!) -> Void in

            if (error == nil) {
                //---get the content of the file and return as NSData---
                var imgData = NSData(contentsOfURL: imgURL!)

                //---get the shared app group URL---
                var fileManager = NSFileManager.defaultManager()
                var storeUrl = fileManager.
                    containerURLForSecurityApplicationGroupIdentifier(
                        "group.learningwatchkit.webservices.app")

                //---save the file using this name---
                var fileURL =
                    storeUrl?.URLByAppendingPathComponent("image.png")

                //---save the file to the shared app group---
                imgData?.writeToURL(fileURL!, atomically: true)
            }
            else {
                println("Error: \(error.localizedDescription)")
            }
    })
}

func pickerView(pickerView: UIPickerView, didSelectRow row: Int,
    inComponent component: Int) {
        var defaults = NSUserDefaults(suiteName:
            "group.learningwatchkit.webservices.app")
        defaults?.setObject(countries[row], forKey: "country")
        defaults?.synchronize()
```

```
//---download the flag of the country selected---
switch countries[row] {
case "Singapore": downloadImage(
    "https://dl.dropboxusercontent.com/u/" +
    "37098169/Flags/flag_singapore.png")
case "Norway": downloadImage(
    "https://dl.dropboxusercontent.com/u/" +
    "37098169/Flags/flag_norway.png")
case "Japan": downloadImage(
    "https://dl.dropboxusercontent.com/u/" +
    "37098169/Flags/flag_japan.png")
case "Thailand": downloadImage(
    "https://dl.dropboxusercontent.com/u/" +
    "37098169/Flags/flag_thailand.png")
case "Hong Kong": downloadImage(
    "https://dl.dropboxusercontent.com/u/" +
    "37098169/Flags/flag_hong_kong.png")
default: break;
}
```

    }

In the previous code:

- You had a method named `downloadImage:`, which takes in a string containing the URL of the image (flag of the selected country) that you want to download.

- You use the `NSURLConnection` class to asynchronously download the image from the specified URL.

- To save the image file in the shared app group, you need to use the `containerURLForSecurityApplicationGroupIdentifier` method of an `NSFileManager` object to obtain the path of the shared app group, passing it the shared group name that you created in the previous section.

- You then save the image in the shared app group, with the name image.png.

- You will download the image every time the user changes the country in the Picker view.

2. Add an Image control to the Interface Controller in the Interface.storyboard file (see Figure 4.52). Set its attributes as follows:

- Horizontal: **Center**
- Width: **Fixed, 30**
- Height: **Fixed, 30**

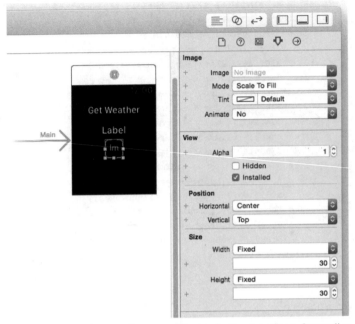

Figure 4.52   Adding an Image control onto the Interface Controller

3. Create an outlet for the Image control. This creates the following statements in bold in the InterfaceController.swift file located in the extension target:

```
import WatchKit
import Foundation

class InterfaceController: WKInterfaceController {

    @IBOutlet weak var label: WKInterfaceLabel!
    @IBOutlet weak var image: WKInterfaceImage!
```

4. Add the following statements in bold to the InterfaceController.swift file:

```
import WatchKit
import Foundation

class InterfaceController: WKInterfaceController {

    @IBOutlet weak var label: WKInterfaceLabel!
    @IBOutlet weak var image: WKInterfaceImage!

    @IBAction func btnGetWeather() {

        var defaults = NSUserDefaults(suiteName:
            "group.learningwatchkit.webservices.app")
```

```
//---send the country to the iOS app---
var country = defaults?.objectForKey("country") as! String
let dataToPhone = [
    "country" : country,
]


WKInterfaceController.openParentApplication(dataToPhone) {
    (replyDataFromPhone, error) -> Void in
    if replyDataFromPhone != nil {
        //---extract the temperature from the result returned by the
        // iOS app---
        var temperature = replyDataFromPhone["temp"] as! Double
        var temperatureStr = String(format:"%.2f", temperature)

        self.label.setText("Temperature in " + country +
            " is \(temperatureStr) Degrees Celsius")

        //---get the shared app group URL---
        var fileManager = NSFileManager.defaultManager()
        var storeUrl = fileManager.
            containerURLForSecurityApplicationGroupIdentifier(
                "group.learningwatchkit.webservices.app")
        var fileURL = storeUrl?.URLByAppendingPathComponent("image.png")

        //---load the file into NSData---
        var imgData = NSData(contentsOfURL: fileURL!)
        if imgData != nil {
            //---display the image---
            self.image.setImageData(imgData)
        }
    } else {
        self.label.setText("Error")
    }
}
}
```

In the previous code

- You try to locate the image file located in the shared app group
- If the file is available, you display it in the Image control

5. Run the application on the iPhone Simulator. Launch the WebServices app on the iPhone Simulator and select a country. Next, click the **Get Weather** button on the Apple Watch and observe the information and the image displayed (see Figure 4.53).

Figure 4.53   The iPhone Simulator displaying the image
downloaded by the containing iOS app

Summary

In this chapter, you learned about localizing your watch application and how the watch
application can communicate with the containing iOS app to perform long-running
tasks. In addition, you learned how to share data between the watch application and
the iOS application. In the next chapter, you learn how to handle notifications on your
iPhone and then display the notifications on the Apple Watch.

5

Displaying Notifications

Innovation distinguishes between a leader and a follower.
Steve Jobs

By design, the Apple Watch is an extension of your iPhone. Instead of pulling the iPhone out of your pocket, Apple wants you to look at and perform most of the tasks on your Apple Watch. One of the most common ways a user interacts with the iPhone is through notifications, and the Apple Watch supports that right out of the box.

When an iPhone is paired with an Apple Watch, notifications received by the iPhone will be sent to the Apple Watch. Your Apple Watch application can then have the option to display the notification to the user in more detail, and you can also accomplish actions associated with the notifications.

What Is a Notification?

A notification in iOS is a message that informs the user of some information that is coming in. For example, the Messages application may display a notification to inform you that you have an incoming message from a friend, or you may receive a notification informing you that you have a new email message on your mail server. Notifications allow applications that are not running in the foreground notify the user of new data, and they allow app developers to write useful applications that work even if an application is in the background.

On iOS, a user can receive two types of notifications:

- **Local notifications**: Notifications sent by the app itself. For example, an events-management application may schedule local notifications to be fired at different times to remind users of upcoming events.

- **Remote notifications** (also commonly known as *push notifications*): Notifications sent from outside the device. For example, a chat application sends a notification to a user when someone sends the user a message.

In iOS 8, Apple added interactive notifications so that you can directly act on a notification when you receive it. A good example is Gmail on the iPhone. The left panel of Figure 5.1 shows a notification about a new email message when the device is unlocked; the notification is shown as a banner at the top of the screen. If you touch the notification and drag it downward, you see two action buttons: Reply and Archive (see Figure 5.1, right).

Tapping the **Reply** button brings the Gmail application to the foreground so that you can reply to that email message. Tapping the **Archive** button directly archives the message without bringing Gmail to the foreground. An action button that brings the application to the foreground is known as a *foreground* action. Likewise, an action button that does not bring the application to the foreground is known as a *background* action. For both types of action buttons, you can configure whether the user must unlock the device before it performs the action.

Figure 5.1   Receiving a notification from Gmail when the device is unlocked

Figure 5.2 shows the same notification received when the device is locked. Swiping the notification to the left reveals the two action buttons. The action button that performs destructive operations (such as deletion, archiving, etc.) is displayed in red.

When the notification is displayed as a banner, at most two action buttons will be shown.

Figure 5.2   Receiving the notification when the device is locked

To display more than two action buttons, the notification must be configured to display as an alert. Figure 5.3 shows the same notification configured to display as an alert. Tapping the **Options** button (Figure 5.3, left) displays another alert with the various action buttons (Figure 5.3, right).

Here, you see the three action buttons (the first two of which you have already seen): Open, Archive, and Reply.

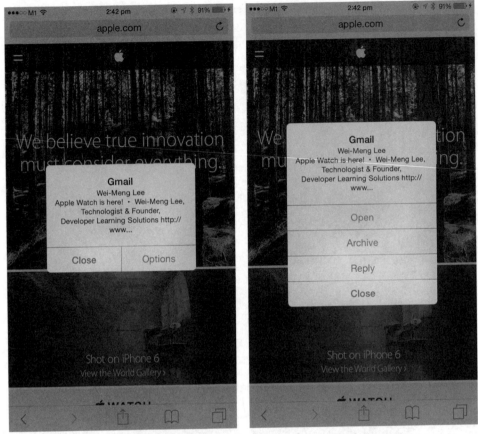

Figure 5.3   Displaying the notification as an alert

For this chapter, remember the following points on iOS Notifications:

- Local notifications emanate from the application itself.
- Remote notification is sent from outside the device.
- An action button can be either a foreground or background action.
- An action button can be configured to perform an action only if the device is unlocked.
- An action button that performs destructive operations is displayed in red.

Types of Notifications on the Apple Watch

When notifications (local or remote) are received on the iPhone, iOS will decide whether to display the notification on the iPhone or send it to the Apple Watch.

When the Apple Watch receives the notification, it will notify the user as follows:

- First it displays the notification using a minimal interface, known as the *short-look interface*. The notification will disappear when the user lowers his wrist.
- If the user's wrist remains raised or if he taps the short-look interface, the *long-look interface* appears. The long-look interface displays the notification in more detail.

Note

If the iPhone is unlocked when a notification arrives, iOS assumes that the iPhone is being used and the notification will show on the iPhone. If the device is locked when the notification arrives, the notification will go to the Apple Watch instead.

For the short-look interface, you don't have to do much, as the interface is pretty restricted—you can just display the content of the notification. For the long-look interface, you can customize the details of the notification by displaying additional text or images.

Implementing the Short-Look Interface

Let's look at how to implement the short-look interface for notifications:

1. Using Xcode, create a new Single View Application project and name it **Notifications**.
2. Add a WatchKit App target to the project. For this project, be sure to check the **Include Notification Scene** option (see Figure 5.4).

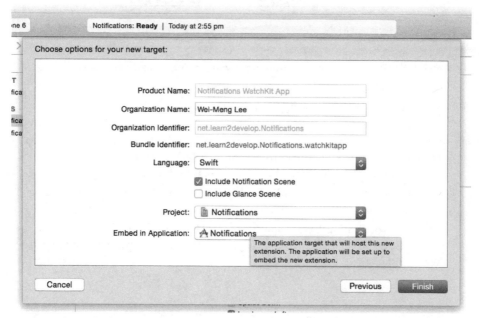

Figure 5.4   Adding a WatchKit App target with the Notification scene to the project

3. Examine the Interface.storyboard file located in the WatchKit app (see Figure 5.5). Observe that, in addition to the Interface Controller, you now have two more controllers: Static Interface Controller and Dynamic Interface Controller.

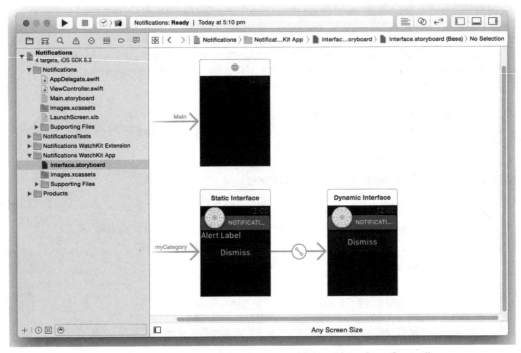

Figure 5.5   The storyboard with the two additional Interface Controllers

The Static Interface Controller is for displaying the short-look interface, whereas the Dynamic Interface Controller is for displaying the long-look interface. Observe that the Static Interface Controller contains a Label control as well as a Dismiss button. The Label control is customizable, whereas the Dismiss button is not (you cannot remove it; neither can you edit its attributes).

4. Examine the PushNotificationPayload.apns file located in the extension project (see Figure 5.6).

The PushNotificationPayload.apns file contains the payload of a remote notification. It is used for simulating receiving a remote (push) notification on the Apple Watch Simulator.

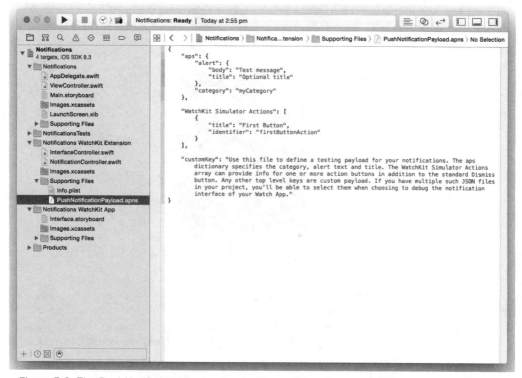

Figure 5.6 The PushNotificationPayload.apns file contains the payload of a remote notification

> **Note**
>
> For testing on the Apple Watch Simulator, notifications received by the iPhone Simulator are not sent to the Apple Watch Simulator; instead, you have to use the PushNotificationPayload.apns file to simulate receiving a remote notification.

5. To test the application, select the **Notification – Notifications WatchKit App** scheme (see Figure 5.7) at the top of Xcode and run it on the iPhone Simulator.

Figure 5.7   Selecting the notification scheme so that the payload can be used for the notification

6. You should see the Apple Watch Simulator displaying the notification, as shown in Figure 5.8.

Figure 5.8 Displaying the notification on the Apple Watch

Observe that the Label control displays the text Test Message, and the button displays the title First Button; both texts come from the PushNotificationPayload.apns file. The Dismiss button is always there, and clicking it dismisses the notification. Clicking **First Button** invokes the default Interface Controller on the WatchKit application.

Customizing the Notification Message

The Label control on the Static Interface Controller supports text containing line break characters (\n). You can use this to break a long line into multiple shorter lines:

1. Using the same project created in the previous section, modify the PushNotification-Payload.apns file as follows:

```
{
    "aps": {
        "alert": {
            "body":
            "Boarding Now\nFlight 164 to Los Angeles boards at 6:50AM at Gate 46",
        },
        "category": "myCategory"
    },

    "WatchKit Simulator Actions": [
        {
            "title": "First Button",
            "identifier": "firstButtonAction"
        }
    ],
```

```
    "customKey": "Use this file to define a testing payload for your
notifications. The aps dictionary specifies the category, alert text, and
title. The WatchKit Simulator Actions array can provide info for one or
more action buttons in addition to the standard Dismiss button. Any other
top level keys are custom payload. If you have multiple such JSON files
in your project, you'll be able to select them when choosing to debug the
notification interface of your Watch App."
}
```

2. In the Interface.storyboard file, set the Lines attribute of the Label control on the Static Interface Controller to **0** (see Figure 5.9).

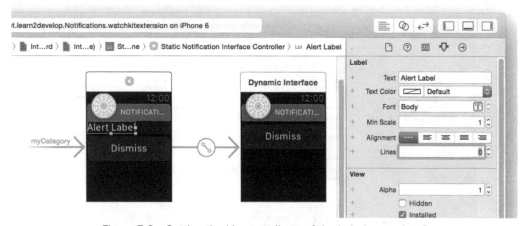

Figure 5.9   Setting the Lines attribute of the Label control to 0

3. Run the application on the iPhone Simulator. You should now see the text on the Label control displayed in multiple lines (see Figure 5.10). To dismiss the notification, you can scroll the page upward and click the **Dismiss** button.

Figure 5.10   The Label control displaying the text broken into multiple lines

Modifying the WatchKit Application Name

If you observe Figure 5.10 carefully, you will notice that the Static Interface Controller is displaying the project name of NOTIFICATION (part of it is truncated). You can change this to display a different name.

1. Select the Info.plist file located in the WatchKit app's Supporting Files group, and modify the value of the Bundle display name key to your desired app name, say, **Apple Air** (see Figure 5.11).

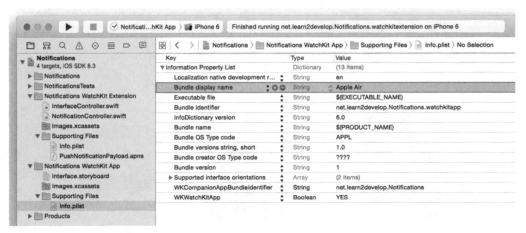

Figure 5.11   Changing the name of the Apple Watch app

2. Run the application on the iPhone simulator, and you should now see the Static Interface Controller showing the display name in all capital letters (see Figure 5.12).

Figure 5.12   The name of the Apple Watch app is now changed

Setting Icons for the Apple Watch App

All Apple Watch apps submitted to the App Store must have icons. To do that, you need to prepare an icon in various sizes and then copy it into your project. These icons are then used in various places on the watch: Notification Center, Apple Watch Companion Settings, Home screen, short-look interface, and long-look interface.

1. Prepare a set of icons with the following names and dimensions:

   - **icon48x48.png**: 48x48 pixels
   - **icon55x55.png**: 55x55 pixels
   - **icon58x58.png**: 58x58 pixels
   - **icon87x87.png**: 87x87 pixels
   - **icon80x80.png**: 80x80 pixels
   - **icon88x88.png**: 88x88 pixels
   - **icon172x172.png**: 172x172 pixels
   - **icon196x196.png**: 196x196 pixels

   > **Note**
   >
   > You can find a copy of these images in the source code download for this book.

2. Select the **Images.xcassets** item in the WatchKit App and drag and drop the icons prepared in the previous steps onto each of the placeholders as shown in Figure 5.13 (follow the order as listed in the previous step).

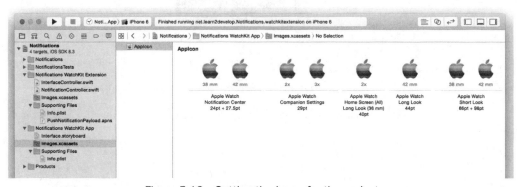

Figure 5.13   Setting the icons for the project

3. In the Interface.storyboard file, observe that the Static Interface Controller and Dynamic Interface Controller now display the icons (see Figure 5.14).

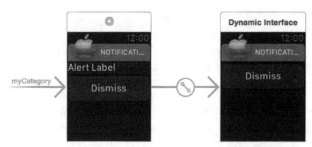

Figure 5.14   The Interface Controllers now show the icon

4. Run the application on the iPhone Simulator. You should now see the icon on the Static Interface Controller (see Figure 5.15).

Figure 5.15   The icon showing on the Static Interface Controller

Setting Background Images

You can also display a background image on the Static Interface Controller.

1. Drag and drop an image named **background.png** onto the Images.xcassets file (see Figure 5.16):

Figure 5.16   Adding an image to the project

2. Select the Static Interface Controller in the Interface.storyboard file and set its Background attribute to **background** (see Figure 5.17). Also, set its Mode attribute to **Aspect Fit**.

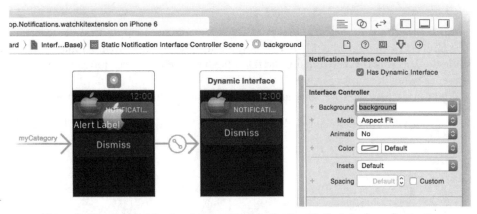

Figure 5.17   Setting the background image for the Static Interface Controller

3. Run the application on the iPhone Simulator. You should now see the background image on the Static Interface Controller (see Figure 5.18).

Figure 5.18   The background image on the Static Interface Controller

Action Buttons

Earlier, you saw that the PushNotificationPayload.apns file contains the payload of a remote notification. In the WatchKit Simulator Actions key, you saw that you have a single item titled First Button with the identifier of firstButtonAction:

```
"WatchKit Simulator Actions": [
    {
        "title": "First Button",
        "identifier": "firstButtonAction"
    }
],
```

This item simulates that your remote notification contains a single action button. The `title` key contains the title of the button to display in the short-look interface while the `identifier` key contains the ID of the button that you can programmatically reference when the button is tapped.

You can simulate your remote notification containing multiple action buttons:

1. Modify/add the following statements in bold to the PushNotificationPayload.apns file:

```
{
    "aps": {
        "alert": {
            "body":
            "Boarding Now\nFlight 164 to Los Angeles boards at 6:50AM at Gate 46",
        },
        "category": "myCategory"
    },

    "WatchKit Simulator Actions": [
        {
            "title": "Itinerary",
            "identifier": "btnItinerary"
        },
        {
            "title": "Weather",
            "identifier": "btnWeather",
        },
        {
            "title": "Cancel Boarding",
            "identifier": "btnCancel",
            "destructive": 1
        },
    ],

    "customKey": "Use this file to define a testing payload for your
    notifications. The aps dictionary specifies the category, alert text, and
    title. The WatchKit Simulator Actions array can provide info for one or
    more action buttons in addition to the standard Dismiss button. Any other
    top level keys are custom payload. If you have multiple such JSON files
    in your project, you'll be able to select them when choosing to debug the
    notification interface of your Watch App."
}
```

The `destructive` key with a value of 1 indicates that this action button is a destructive one.

2. Run the application on the iPhone Simulator. Observe that the short-look interface now displays four buttons (including the Dismiss button), with the destructive action button displayed in red (see Figure 5.19).

Figure 5.19   The Static Interface Controller displaying four buttons

Note

Realistically, the short-look interface is short-lived—the user does not have much time to look at the screen and tap the buttons before the short-look interface transitions to the long-look interface.

Handling the Action Buttons

As described at the beginning of this chapter, a notification can contain action buttons. There are two types of action buttons: foreground and background. When a notification is received and displayed on the iPhone, a foreground action button will launch the iPhone application and bring it to the foreground, whereas a background action button will launch the iPhone application and execute in the background.

On the Apple Watch

- A foreground action button fires either the `handleActionWithIdentifier:-forLocalNotification:` (for local notifications) or `handleActionWith-Identifier:forRemoteNotification:` (for remote notifications) method of the main Interface Controller for your Watch app

- A background action button fires either the `application:handleAction-WithIdentifier:forLocalNotification:` (for local notifications) or the `application:handleActionWithIdentifier:forRemoteNotification:` (for remote notifications) method in the containing iOS app

1. In the Interface.storyboard file, add two Label controls onto the Interface Controller (see Figure 5.20). Set the Lines attributes of both Label controls to **0**.

Figure 5.20   Adding two Label controls to the Interface Controller

2. Create two outlets for the Label controls. This adds the following statements in bold to the InterfaceController.swift file:

```
import WatchKit
import Foundation

class InterfaceController: WKInterfaceController {

    @IBOutlet weak var label1: WKInterfaceLabel!
    @IBOutlet weak var label2: WKInterfaceLabel!
    override func awakeWithContext(context: AnyObject?) {
        super.awakeWithContext(context)
```

3. In the PushNotificationPayload.apns file, add the following statements in bold:

```
{
    "aps": {
        "alert": {
            "body":
            "Boarding Now\nFlight 164 to Los Angeles boards at 6:50AM at Gate 46",
        },
        "category": "myCategory"
    },

    "WatchKit Simulator Actions": [
        {
            "title": "Itinerary",
            "identifier": "btnItinerary"
        },
        {
            "title": "Weather",
            "identifier": "btnWeather",
        },
```

```
        {
            "title": "Cancel Boarding",
            "identifier": "btnCancel",
            "destructive": 1
        },
    ],

    "gateclose":"7:30AM",

    "customKey": "Use this file to define a testing payload for your
notifications. The aps dictionary specifies the category, alert text, and
title. The WatchKit Simulator Actions array can provide info for one or
more action buttons in addition to the standard Dismiss button. Any other
top level keys are custom payload. If you have multiple such JSON files
in your project, you'll be able to select them when choosing to debug the
notification interface of your Watch App."
}
```

4. Add the following statements in bold to the **InterfaceController.swift** file:

```
import WatchKit
import Foundation

class InterfaceController: WKInterfaceController {

    @IBOutlet weak var label1: WKInterfaceLabel!
    @IBOutlet weak var label2: WKInterfaceLabel!

    override func awakeWithContext(context: AnyObject?) {
        super.awakeWithContext(context)

        // Configure interface objects here.
        label1.setText("")
        label2.setText("")
    }

    func handleButtons (btnIdentifier : String) {
        switch btnIdentifier {
        case "btnItinerary":
            label2.setText("Arriving in Los Angeles at 11:50AM")
        case "btnWeather":
            label2.setText("The weather in Los Angeles is 62 degrees")
        case "btnCancel":
            label2.setText("Please proceed to the gate immediately.")
        default:break
        }
    }
```

```
//---fired when a foreground action button in a location notification
// is tapped---
override func handleActionWithIdentifier(identifier: String?,
forLocalNotification localNotification: UILocalNotification) {
    handleButtons(identifier!)
}

//---fired when a foreground action button in a remote notification
// is tapped---
override func handleActionWithIdentifier(identifier: String?,
forRemoteNotification remoteNotification: [NSObject : AnyObject]) {
    if let s = remoteNotification["gateclose"] as? String {
        label1.setText("Gate Close: \(s)")
    }
    handleButtons(identifier!)
}
```

The first argument of the `handleActionWithIdentifier:forRemote-Notification:` method passes in the identifier of the action button. The second argument passes in a copy of the notification received. Here, you can retrieve the content and use it to get the time the gate closes.

> **Note**
>
> The main entry point for your Watch application (which is of type WKInterface-Controller) will handle all foreground actions of the notifications. The handling is not performed at the Notification Controller.

5. Run the application on the iPhone Simulator and click one of the buttons shown on the Apple Watch Simulator (see Figure 5.21). You should see the main Interface Controller launch, showing the details of the notification.

Figure 5.21   Clicking any of the action buttons launches
the default Interface Controller on the Watch app

6. For background actions, you need to implement the `application:handle-ActionWithIdentifier:forLocalNotification:` and the `application:handleActionWithIdentifier:forRemoteNotification:` methods in the containing iOS app. Add the following statements in bold to the AppDelegate .swift file:

```swift
import UIKit

@UIApplicationMain
class AppDelegate: UIResponder, UIApplicationDelegate {

    var window: UIWindow?

    func handleButtons (btnIdentifier : String) {
        //...
    }

    //---fired when a background action button in a location notification
    // is tapped---
    func application(application: UIApplication,
    handleActionWithIdentifier identifier: String?,
    forLocalNotification notification: UILocalNotification,
    completionHandler: () -> Void) {
        handleButtons(identifier!)
    }

    //---fired when a background action button in a remote notification
    // is tapped---
    func application(application: UIApplication,
    handleActionWithIdentifier identifier: String?,
    forRemoteNotification userInfo: [NSObject : AnyObject],
    completionHandler: () -> Void) {
        handleButtons(identifier!)
    }
}
```

Note

You can only test the above on an actual iOS device and Apple Watch.

Implementing the Long-Look Interface

When the user taps the short-look interface or continues keeping his wrist raised, the long-look interface appears. The long-look interface allows you to display the notification in more detail (such as using additional Label and Image controls). However, interactions are still not allowed with the user, apart from the action buttons and the dismiss button. This means that you cannot add your own Button to the long-look interface.

1. Add the following statements in bold to the PushNotificationPayload.apns file:

```
{
    "aps": {
        "alert": {
            "body":
            "Boarding Now\nFlight 164 to Los Angeles boards at 6:50AM at Gate 46",
        },
        "category": "myCategory"
    },
    "status"   : "Boarding",
    "flight"   : "164",
    "time"     : "6:50AM",
    "gate"     : "46",
    "gateclose": "7:30AM",
    "WatchKit Simulator Actions": [
        {
            "title": "Itinerary",
            "identifier": "btnItinerary"
        },
        {
            "title": "Weather",
            "identifier": "btnWeather",
        },
        {
            "title": "Cancel Boarding",
            "identifier": "btnCancel",
            "destructive": 1
        },
    ],

    "customKey": "Use this file to define a testing payload for your
notifications. The aps dictionary specifies the category, alert text, and
title. The WatchKit Simulator Actions array can provide info for one or
more action buttons in addition to the standard Dismiss button. Any other
top level keys are custom payload. If you have multiple such JSON files
in your project, you'll be able to select them when choosing to debug the
notification interface of your Watch App."
}
```

The previous statements simulate the notification containing the additional information about a particular flight.

2. In the Interface.storyboard file, add an Image control and three Label controls to the Dynamic Interface Controller (see Figure 5.22). For each of the four controls, set the Horizontal attribute to **Center**. Also, set the Lines attribute for each of the Label controls to **0**.

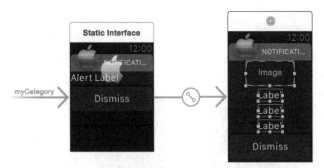

Figure 5.22   Adding four controls to the Dynamic Interface Controller

3. Drag and drop two images named boarding.png and info.png into the Images.
xcassets file located in the WatchKit app (see Figure 5.23).

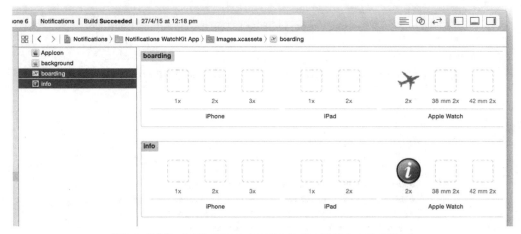

Figure 5.23   Adding more images to the Watch app project

4. Examine the Dynamic Interface Controller and observe from its Identity Inspector window that its Class is set to NotificationController (see Figure 5.24). This
class is represented by the NotificationController.swift file located in the extension project.

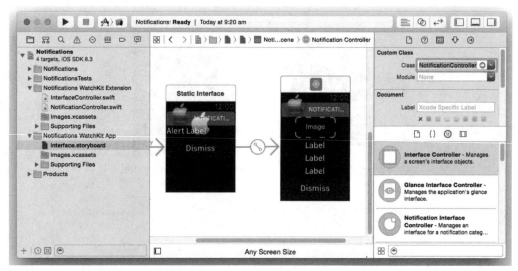

Figure 5.24   The class representing the Dynamic Interface Controller

5. Create outlets for the Image and Label controls in the NotificationController.swift file:

```
import WatchKit
import Foundation

class NotificationController: WKUserNotificationInterfaceController {

    @IBOutlet weak var image: WKInterfaceImage!
    @IBOutlet weak var lblBody: WKInterfaceLabel!
    @IBOutlet weak var lblGate: WKInterfaceLabel!
    @IBOutlet weak var lblTime: WKInterfaceLabel!

    override init() {
        // Initialize variables here.
        super.init()

        // Configure interface objects here.
    }
```

6. Add the following statements in bold to the NotificationController.swift file:

```
import WatchKit
import Foundation

class NotificationController: WKUserNotificationInterfaceController {
```

```swift
@IBOutlet weak var image: WKInterfaceImage!
@IBOutlet weak var lblGate: WKInterfaceLabel!
@IBOutlet weak var lblTime: WKInterfaceLabel!

override init() {
    // Initialize variables here.
    super.init()

    // Configure interface objects here.
}

override func willActivate() {
    // This method is called when watch view controller is about to
    // be visible to user
    super.willActivate()
}

override func didDeactivate() {
    // This method is called when watch view controller is no longer
    // visible
    super.didDeactivate()
}

override func didReceiveLocalNotification(localNotification:
UILocalNotification, withCompletion completionHandler:
((WKUserNotificationInterfaceType) -> Void)) {
    // This method is called when a local notification needs to be
    // presented.
    // Implement it if you use a dynamic notification interface.
    // Populate your dynamic notification interface as quickly as
    // possible.
    //
    // After populating your dynamic notification interface call the
    // completion block.
    completionHandler(.Custom)
}

override func didReceiveRemoteNotification(remoteNotification:
[NSObject : AnyObject], withCompletion completionHandler:
((WKUserNotificationInterfaceType) -> Void)) {
    // This method is called when a remote notification needs to be
    // presented.
    // Implement it if you use a dynamic notification interface.
    // Populate your dynamic notification interface as quickly as
    // possible.
    //
    // After populating your dynamic notification interface call the
    // completion block.
```

```
let alert = remoteNotification["aps"]!["alert"]! as! NSDictionary
self.lblBody.setText(alert["body"]! as? String)

if remoteNotification["status"] as! String == "Boarding" {
    self.image.setImageNamed("boarding")
} else if remoteNotification["status"] as! String == "Delayed" {
    self.image.setImageNamed("info")
}

self.lblGate.setText("Gate: " +
    (remoteNotification["gate"] as! String))
self.lblTime.setText("Boarding: " + (remoteNotification["time"] as!
    String))
completionHandler(.Custom)
    }

}
```

To implement the long-look interface, you need to implement the above two methods in the `NotificationController` class:

- `didReceiveLocalNotification:withCompletion:` fired when a local notification is received

- `didReceiveRemoteNotification:withCompletion:` fired when a remote notification is received

In both methods, you should perform your task quickly. If they take a long time to execute, the Apple Watch will default back to the short-look interface. At the end of the method, you have to call the completion handler, `completionHandler`, by passing it an enumeration of type `WKUserNotificationInterfaceType`. Typically, you use `Custom`, but you can also use `Default` to default back to the short-look interface if the payload does not contain what you expected.

Because the Apple Watch Simulator only simulates remote notification, add the code in the `didReceiveRemoteNotification:withCompletion:` method to extract the flight details from the notification payload and display the extra details on the Image and Label controls.

> **Note**
>
> For testing on the Apple Simulator, if you implement the `didReceiveRemote-Notification:withCompletion:` method and return `Custom` for the completion handler, the Dynamic Interface Controller is displayed when you run the app on the iPhone Simulator. Otherwise, the Static Interface Controller will always load.

7. Run the application on the iPhone Simulator. You should now see the long-look interface showing the icon and the details of the flight (see Figure 5.25).

Figure 5.25   The Dynamic Interface Controller showing the details of the flight

Simulating Using Different Notification Payloads

Besides the default PushNotificationPayload.apns file included in the extension project for simulating a remote notification, you can also add files to simulate additional
remote notifications:

1. Right-click the **Supporting Files** group of the extension and add a new file.
   Select **Apple Watch | Notification Simulation File** (see Figure 5.26) and
   click **Next**. Name the file **PushNotificationPayload-delayed.apns**.

Figure 5.26   Adding a Notification Simulation File to the project

2. The file should now appear in the Supporting Files group (see Figure 5.27).

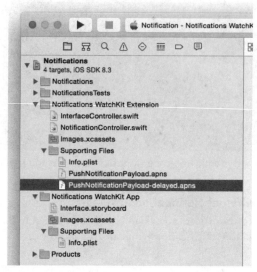

Figure 5.27   The newly added payload file

3. Populate the PushNotificationPayload–delayed.apns file as follows:

> **Note**
>
> The value of the `body` key in the PushNotificationPayload-delayed.apns file has
> been formatted for readability. When testing on the iPhone Simulator, it should be a
> continuous line—"Flight Delayed\nFlight 164 to Los Angeles now boards at 7:50AM
> at Gate 56".

```
{
    "aps": {
        "alert": {
            "body": "Flight Delayed\nFlight 164 to Los Angeles now
                    boards at 7:50AM at Gate 56",
        },
        "category": "myCategory"
    },
    "status": "Delayed",
    "flight" :"164",
    "time": "7:50AM",
    "gate": "56",
    "gateclose":"8:30AM",
```

```
"WatchKit Simulator Actions": [
    {
        "title": "Itinerary",
        "identifier": "btnItinerary"
    },
    {
        "title": "Weather",
        "identifier": "btnWeather",
    },
    {
        "title": "Cancel Boarding",
        "identifier": "btnCancel",
        "destructive": 1
    },
]
}
```

4. To select the newly added payload file for testing, select the **Edit Scheme...** item located at the top of Xcode (see Figure 5.28).

Figure 5.28   Editing the scheme to run the project

5. In the Run configuration, select **PushNotificationPayload-delayed.apns** as the Notification Payload (see Figure 5.29).

6. Run the application on the iPhone Simulator. You should now see the long-look interface showing a different set of icons and details of the flight (see Figure 5.30).

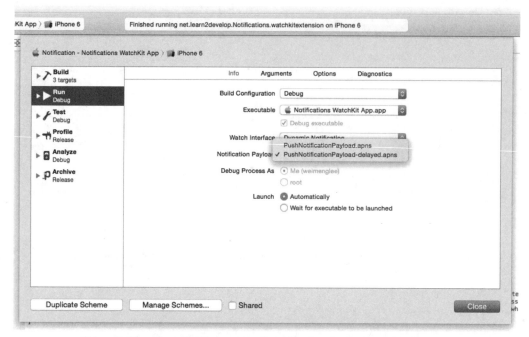

Figure 5.29   Choosing the new payload file for simulating a notification

Figure 5.30   The Dynamic Interface Controller showing the details of the new notification

Changing Sash Color

Both the Static Interface Controller and the Dynamic Interface Controller allow you to change their sash colors and title colors.

1. Select the **myCategory** arrow in the Interface.storyboard file and, in the Attributes Inspector window, change its Sash Color to **Yellow** and Title Color to **Blue** (see Figure 5.31). You should immediately see the changes in color.

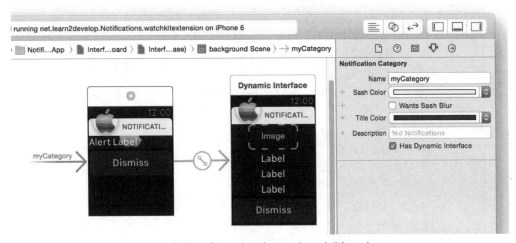

Figure 5.31   Changing the sash and title colors

2. Run the application on the iPhone Simulator, and observe the sash and title colors in the Dynamic Interface Controller (see Figure 5.32).

Figure 5.32   The sash and title colors are now changed

Simulating Delays in Displaying the Dynamic Interface Controller

If the Dynamic Interface Controller takes a long time to display, the Apple Watch will revert back to the Static Interface Controller:

1. To prove this, add the following statement in bold to the NotificationController .swift file:

```
override func didReceiveRemoteNotification(remoteNotification: [NSObject :
AnyObject], withCompletion completionHandler:
((WKUserNotificationInterfaceType) -> Void)) {
    // This method is called when a remote notification needs to be
    // presented.
    // Implement it if you use a dynamic notification interface.
    // Populate your dynamic notification interface as quickly as possible.
    //
    // After populating your dynamic notification interface call the
    // completion block.

    //---insert a 10 second delay---
    sleep(10)

    let alert = remoteNotification["aps"]!["alert"]! as! NSDictionary
    self.lblBody.setText(alert["body"]! as? String)

    if remoteNotification["status"] as! String == "Boarding" {
        self.image.setImageNamed("boarding.png")
    } else if remoteNotification["status"] as! String == "Delayed" {
        self.image.setImageNamed("info.png")
    }

    self.lblGate.setText("Gate: " +
        (remoteNotification["gate"] as? String)!)
    self.lblTime.setText("Boarding: " + (remoteNotification["time"] as?
        String)!)

    completionHandler(.Custom)
}
```

2. Run the application on the iPhone Simulator. In the Output window, an error message that says, "Took too long to show custom notification. Falling back to static." appears, and the Apple Watch Simulator displays the Static Interface Controller.

Summary

In this chapter, you learned how to implement notifications in your Apple Watch apps. You learned about the different types of notifications and how they are handled in the Apple Watch. You also saw how to simulate notifications with different payloads. In the next chapter, you learn how to implement glances in your Apple Watch apps.

6

Displaying Glances

*Every good product I've ever seen is because a group of people cared
deeply about making something wonderful that they and their friends
wanted. They wanted to use it themselves.*

Steve Jobs

Most people interact with their watches by *glancing* at the watch to check the time. For
the Apple Watch, Apple has extended this traditional form of interaction by providing
glances for your watch applications. Instead of just glancing for the time, users can have
a quick glance at the state of the various applications. Glances are shown when users
swipe up from the watch. The Apple Watch then shows a scrollable list of glances from
apps that support them (up to a maximum of 20 glances). Think of glances as snapshots
of the various apps on the watch: Instagram may show the most recently shared photo,
while Twitter may show the latest trending tweets. Glances provide the user with a
quick summary of information that may be important to him. If the user wants more
details, tapping a glance launches the corresponding watch app.

If your app supports glances, you need to add a Glance scene to your storyboard file.
Each user needs to manually turn on the glance of your application through the Apple
Watch application on his watch.

In this chapter, you learn how to implement glances for your Apple Watch apps.

What Is a Glance?

From a developer's perspective, a glance is an additional avenue for your app to display
a quick summary of information to the user. Imagine an iPhone app that fetches stock
prices at regular time intervals. A user who wants to have a quick look at the price of
a particular stock can simply swipe up from the watch face and view the most recently
fetched price of the stock. This can be done without launching your app. Of course,
if the user wants to view more detailed information, he can tap the glance to launch
the app.

Implementing Glances

Let's look at how to implement a glance for an application:

1. Using Xcode, create a new Single View Application project and name it **DisplayingGlances**.

2. Add a WatchKit App target to the project. For this project, be sure to uncheck the Include Notification Scene option and check the Include Glance Scene option (see Figure 6.1).

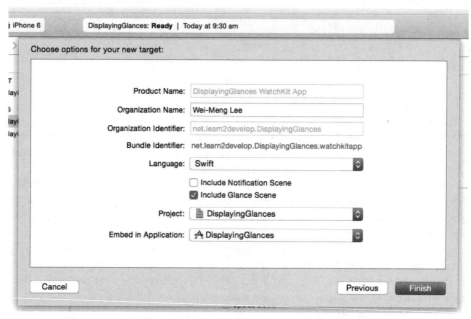

Figure 6.1   Adding the WatchKit App target with the Glance Scene

3. In the WatchKit app, select the Interface.storyboard file. You should now see the Glance Interface Controller together with the Interface Controller (see Figure 6.2).

> **Note**
>
> Each Apple Watch app can contain at most one Glance Interface Controller.

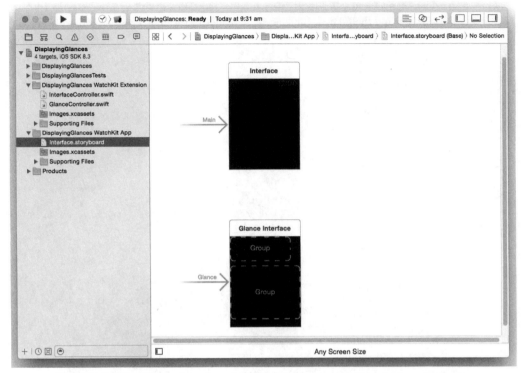

Figure 6.2   The Glance Interface Controller together with the Interface Controller

4. In the Extension project, you see the GlanceController.swift file (see Figure 6.3).

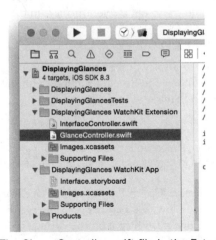

Figure 6.3   The GlanceController.swift file in the Extension project

5. The GlanceController.swift file contains the `GlanceController` class, which is representing the Glance Interface Controller in the Interface.storyboard file:

```
import WatchKit
import Foundation

class GlanceController: WKInterfaceController {

    override func awakeWithContext(context: AnyObject?) {
        super.awakeWithContext(context)

        // Configure interface objects here.
    }

    override func willActivate() {
        // This method is called when watch view controller is about to be
        // visible to user
        super.willActivate()
    }

    override func didDeactivate() {
        // This method is called when watch view controller is no longer
        // visible
        super.didDeactivate()
    }

}
```

Observe that the `GlanceController` class extends the `WKInterfaceController` class, the same as the Interface Controller. The same Interface Controller lifecycle applies to the Glance Controller as well. The only exception is that, for a Glance Controller, the initialization takes place very early so that the information can be quickly displayed. Hence, you should try to update your glances in the `willActivate` method.

Customizing the Glance

Glances can be customized to display different types of information. However, like notifications, users are not allowed to have interactions with the glances. This means that controls, like Button and Slider, are not allowed.

Note

Remember that glances are supposed to show users information quickly. Hence, you should design your glances to convey as much information as quickly as possible.

1. Select the Glance Interface Controller in the Interface.storyboard file and view its Attributes Inspector window (see Figure 6.4). Observe that it is divided into two sections: Upper and Lower. Both contain the Group control, which allows you to add controls like Label and Image.

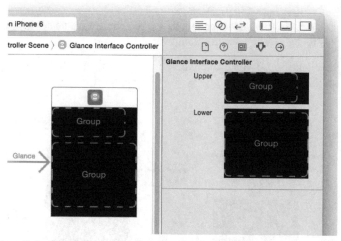

Figure 6.4   The Glance Interface Controller is divided into two sections

2. Click the **Upper** group in the Attributes Inspector window, and you see a drop-down list (see Figure 6.5). This list shows a predefined template showing some of the common designs for the Upper section. Select the bottom-left item.

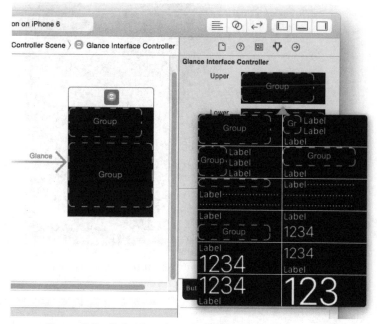

Figure 6.5   Selecting the template for the Upper section

> **Note**
>
> If you do not like the predefined templates, you can always add and lay out your own controls to the Glance Interface Controller.

3. Likewise, click the **Lower** group, and you see a drop-down list (see Figure 6.6). Select the top-left item.

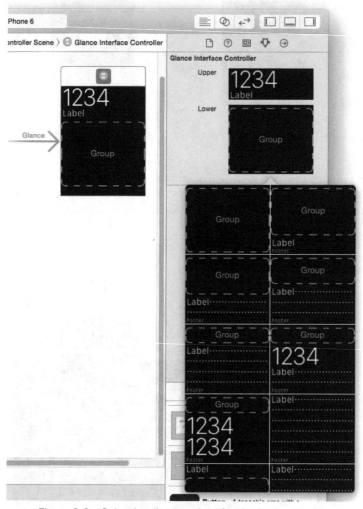

Figure 6.6   Selecting the template for the Lower section

4. Add a Label control to the Lower group (see Figure 6.7) and set its attributes as follows:

- Font: **System Italic**
- Size: **30**
- Text Color: **Yellow**
- Style: **Bold**
- Horizontal: **Center**
- Vertical: **Center**

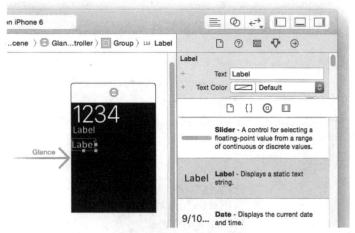

Figure 6.7   Adding a Label control to the Lower section

> **Note**
>
> You can only use the system font (San Francisco) for glances and notifications on the Apple Watch; custom fonts are not supported.

5. The Glance Interface Controller now looks like Figure 6.8.

Figure 6.8   The final design for the Glance Interface Controller

Testing the Glance

To test the glance, you need to use the Glance scheme that was created in Xcode when you added the WatchKit App target:

1. In Xcode, select the **Glance – DisplayingGlances WatchKit App** scheme (see Figure 6.9).

Figure 6.9   Selecting the Glance scheme

2. Run the application on the iPhone Simulator. You now see the glance on the Apple Watch Simulator (see Figure 6.10).

Figure 6.10   Displaying the glance on the Apple Watch Simulator

At this moment, the glance is not doing anything useful. In the next section, you modify the application to display some useful information.

Making the App Useful

To make the glance display useful information, you now must modify the application to do the following:

- Modify the containing iOS app to perform a background fetch. Your iOS app can then perform a network operation even if it is switched to the background.

- In the background fetch, the iOS app connects to a Yahoo web service to fetch the prices of two stocks: AAPL (Apple) and MSFT (Microsoft).

- Once the prices of the two stocks are fetched, they are saved using the NSUser-Defaults settings. These values are saved in a shared app group so that the watch app can also access them.

- In the watch app, retrieve the values saved by the NSUserDefaults settings and then display them in the glance.

Creating a Shared App Group

In order to share data between the Extension project and the watch app, you need to create a shared app group.

> **Note**
>
> Chapter 4, "Interfacing with iOS Apps," discusses how to create a shared app group.

1. Create a shared app group for the iOS app and name it group.learningwatchkit .displayingglances.app. Once created, you see the group appear in the App Groups section of the Capabilities tab of your project (see Figure 6.11).

   > **Note**
   >
   > The app group name must be unique, so you need to enter a unique name for your example.

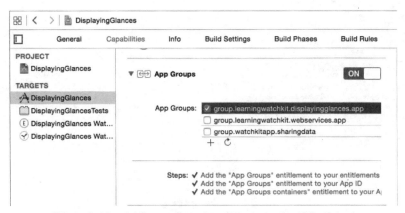

Figure 6.11   Adding a shared app group to the iOS project

2. In the Extension project, check the app group name that you have just added (see Figure 6.12).

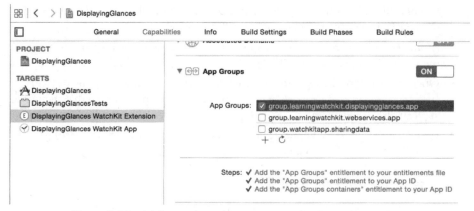

Figure 6.12   Adding a shared app group to the Extension project

Implementing Background Fetch

The containing iOS app connects to the Yahoo web service and downloads the stock prices of Apple and Microsoft when the application is in the background.

1. To implement background fetch on the containing iOS app, select the **Displaying-Glances** target in Xcode and in the Capabilities tab, check the **Background fetch** option under the Background Modes section (see Figure 6.13).

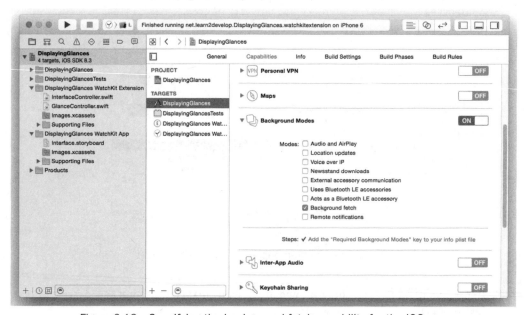

Figure 6.13   Specifying the background fetch capability for the iOS app

2. Add the following statements in bold to the AppDelegate.swift file:

```swift
import UIKit

@UIApplicationMain
class AppDelegate: UIResponder, UIApplicationDelegate {

    var window: UIWindow?

    //---convert from NSDate format to String---
    func currentDateToString() -> String {
        var formatter: NSDateFormatter = NSDateFormatter()
        formatter.dateFormat = "yyyy-MM-dd HH:mm:ss zzz"
        return formatter.stringFromDate(NSDate())
    }

    //---extract the required data from the JSON string---
    func parseJSONData(data: NSData) {
        var error: NSError?
        var parsedJSONData = NSJSONSerialization.JSONObjectWithData(
            data, options: NSJSONReadingOptions.allZeros, error: &error) as!
            [String:AnyObject]
        var query = parsedJSONData["query"] as! [String:AnyObject]

        if let results = query["results"] as? [String:AnyObject] {

            if let quotes = results["quote"] as? [[String:AnyObject]] {
                var defaults = NSUserDefaults(suiteName:
                    "group.learningwatchkit.displayingglances.app")
                for stock in quotes {
                    //---stock symbol---
                    var symbol = stock["symbol"] as! String

                    //---save the asking price and date it was fetched as
                    // a dictionary---
                    var value = ["ask": stock["Ask"] as! String,
                                 "date": currentDateToString()]

                    //---save the stock details into the dictionary---
                    defaults?.setObject(value, forKey: symbol)
                }
                defaults?.synchronize()

            }
        }
    }
```

```
//---performing a background fetch---
func application(application: UIApplication,
performFetchWithCompletionHandler completionHandler:
(UIBackgroundFetchResult) -> Void) {
    var urlString = "http://query.yahooapis.com/v1/public/yql?q=" +
                    "select%20*%20from%20yahoo.finance.quotes%20" +
                    "where%20symbol%20in%20(%22AAPL%22%2C%22MSFT%22)" +
                    "%0A%09%09&env=http%3A%2F%2Fdatatables.org%2" +
                    "Falltables.env&format=json"

    var session = NSURLSession.sharedSession()
    session.dataTaskWithURL(NSURL(string:urlString)!,
        completionHandler: {
            (data, response, error) -> Void in
            var httpResp = response as! NSHTTPURLResponse
            if error == nil && httpResp.statusCode == 200 {
                //---parse the JSON result---
                self.parseJSONData(data)
                completionHandler(UIBackgroundFetchResult.NewData)
            } else {
                completionHandler(UIBackgroundFetchResult.Failed)
            }
    }).resume()
}

func application(application: UIApplication,
didFinishLaunchingWithOptions
launchOptions: [NSObject: AnyObject]?) -> Bool {
    // Override point for customization after application launch.
    UIApplication.sharedApplication().setMinimumBackgroundFetchInterval(
        UIApplicationBackgroundFetchIntervalMinimum)
    return true
}
```

> **Note**
>
> Remember to change the shared group name to the one that you have used.

You just enabled the following to happen:

- You connect to the Yahoo web service to fetch the price of Apple and Microsoft.

- The web service returns the result as a JSON string.

- You pass the JSON string to the parseJSONData: method to extract the relevant data. The following data is extracted: stock symbol and asking price.

- The stock symbol is used as the key to save using the NSUserDefaults settings. The value is the asking price of the stock, plus the date and time the price was fetched. These two pieces of data are saved as a dictionary.

- The `currentDateToString` method returns the current date and time as a `String` object.

- In order to perform a background fetch, you need to call the `setMinimum-BackgroundFetchInterval` method of the `UIApplication` object and pass it the `UIApplicationBackgroundFetchIntervalMinimum` constant.

3. Due to a bug in Xcode 6.3, background fetch does not work correctly on the iPhone Simulator. So, you need to add in the following additional method and statements in the AppDelegate.swift file to manually create the `NSUserDefaults` settings values when the app is loaded:

```
//---temporary fix for Xcode 6's bug in simulating a background fetch---
func temporaryFixForBackgroundFetchOnSimulator() {
    var defaults = NSUserDefaults(suiteName:
        "group.learningwatchkit.displayingglances.app")
    defaults?.setObject(["ask":"131.89",
                         "date":currentDateToString()], forKey: "AAPL")
    defaults?.synchronize()
}

func application(application: UIApplication, didFinishLaunchingWithOptions
launchOptions: [NSObject: AnyObject]?) -> Bool {
    // Override point for customization after application launch.
    UIApplication.sharedApplication().setMinimumBackgroundFetchInterval(
        UIApplicationBackgroundFetchIntervalMinimum)
    temporaryFixForBackgroundFetchOnSimulator()
    return true
}
```

4. Select the **DisplayingGlances** scheme (see Figure 6.14) in Xcode and run the application on the iPhone Simulator.

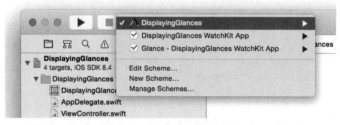

Figure 6.14   Selecting the DisplayingGlances scheme

5. To simulate a background fetch on the application, select **Debug | Simulate Background Fetch** in Xcode.

> **Note**
>
> In Xcode 6.3, background fetch does not work on the iPhone Simulator.

6. The application should now fetch the prices from the web service and save them through the NSUserDefaults settings.

Updating the Glance

Now that the stock prices are downloaded and saved, it is time to display them on the Glance Interface Controller.

1. In the GlanceController.swift file, create three outlets for the three Label controls in the Glance Interface Controller:

```
import WatchKit
import Foundation

class GlanceController: WKInterfaceController {

    @IBOutlet weak var lblSymbol: WKInterfaceLabel!
    @IBOutlet weak var lblLastUpdate: WKInterfaceLabel!
    @IBOutlet weak var lblAsk: WKInterfaceLabel!

    override func awakeWithContext(context: AnyObject?) {
        super.awakeWithContext(context)

        // Configure interface objects here.
    }
```

2. Add the following statements in bold to the GlanceController.swift file:

```
import WatchKit
import Foundation

class GlanceController: WKInterfaceController {

    @IBOutlet weak var lblSymbol: WKInterfaceLabel!
    @IBOutlet weak var lblLastUpdate: WKInterfaceLabel!
    @IBOutlet weak var lblAsk: WKInterfaceLabel!

    override func awakeWithContext(context: AnyObject?) {
        super.awakeWithContext(context)

        // Configure interface objects here.
    }

    //---convert from string to NSDate---
    func dateStringToDate(date:String) -> NSDate {
        var dateFormatter = NSDateFormatter()
```

```
        dateFormatter.dateFormat = "yyyy-MM-dd HH:mm:ss zzz"
        return dateFormatter.dateFromString(date)!
    }


    override func willActivate() {
        // This method is called when watch view controller is about to be
        // visible to user
        super.willActivate()

        var defaults = NSUserDefaults(suiteName:
            "group.learningwatchkit.displayingglances.app")

        //---retrieve the price and date fetched from the settings---
        var priceAndDate = defaults?.objectForKey("AAPL") as! [String:String]
        var price = priceAndDate["ask"]!
        var dateFetched = dateStringToDate(priceAndDate["date"]!)


        //---the difference between the current time and the time the price was
        // fetched---
        let elapsedTime = NSDate().timeIntervalSinceDate(dateFetched)

        //---convert to seconds---
        let elapsedTimeSeconds = Int(elapsedTime)

        //---convert the time to mins and secs---
        let elapsedMin = elapsedTimeSeconds / 60
        let elapsedSec = elapsedTimeSeconds % 60

        if elapsedMin > 0 {
            lblLastUpdate.setText(
            "\(elapsedMin) mins \(Int(elapsedSec)) secs")
        } else {
            lblLastUpdate.setText("\(Int(elapsedTime)) secs")
        }
        //---show the info on the glance---
        self.lblSymbol.setText("AAPL")
        self.lblAsk.setText("$" + price)
    }
```

Note

Remember to change the shared group name to the one that you have used.

You just enabled the following to happen:

- You load the values saved in the NSUserDefaults settings. For simplicity, you are only retrieving one stock price: AAPL. The value of the AAPL key is a dictionary containing the price as well as the date and time it was fetched.

- The `dateStringToDate:` method accepts the date and time as a `String` and then returns an `NSDate` object.

- You calculate the elapsed time since the price was fetched using the `timeIntervalSinceDate:` method of the `NSDate` object.

- You then display the stock symbol, the elapsed time since the price was fetched, and the price of the stock in the Glance Interface Controller.

3. In Xcode, switch to the **Glance – DisplayingGlances WatchKit App** scheme and test the application on the iPhone Simulator. The Glance Interface Controller should now look like Figure 6.15.

Figure 6.15   The glance showing the latest fetched price

Summary

In this chapter, you learned how to implement glances in your Apple Watch application. You also learned how to perform background fetch in your containing iOS application and then display the information downloaded in your Glance Interface Controller.

Index

Symbols
– (minus) button, on Slider control, 62, 64–65
+ (plus) button, on Slider control, 62, 64–65
< (chevron)
    customizing title of, 34–35
    in hierarchical navigation, 26

A
Accessing web services, 126–130
Action buttons
    destructive, 151–152, 163
    displaying multiple, 161–163
    handling, 163–167
    for notifications, 150–152
    types of, 150, 163
Action Segue
    modal selection, 27
    push selection, 24
Animation, performing, 69–71
Apple Developer Program, 131–132
Apple Watch apps. *See also* Application(s)
    icons for, 159–160
    localization of. *See* Localization
    modifying display name of, 158
    sharing files with iOS app, 143–148
    testing, 14–15
    tools for, 2
    types of, 6
Apple Watch Simulator
    app tested on, 14
    Button tested on, 47
    dictation and, 85
    emojis and, 86
    glance displayed on, 186
    location data displayed on, 123
    notification displayed on, 156
    temperature displayed on, 130
    unlocking, 22

Apple Watch specifications, 1–2
ApplicationGroupContainerIdentifier key, 142
application:handleActionWithIdentifier:
    forLocal-Notification: method, 163–167
application:handleActionWithIdentifier:
    forRemote-Notification: method, 163–167
Application(s)
    adding target to, 8–11
    Apple Watch. *See* Apple Watch apps
    creating iPhone, 6–8
Archive button, for notifications, 150–151
Attributed strings
    customizing fonts with, 52–55
    displaying, 51
Attribute(s)
    Background, 59
    for customizing glances, 185
    Identifier, 25, 27, 36–39, 75
    Image control, 79, 95, 145–146
    Label control, 73
    Lines, 156–157
    Menu Item control, 93–94
    Mode, 70
    Selectable, 75, 81
    Slider control, 63–64
    Steps, 64–65
    Vertical, 73
Attributes Inspector window
    Background attribute in, 59
    changing Button title in, 46–47
    changing sash/title color in, 177
    Glance Interface Controller in, 182–183
    hierarchical setting in, 25
    of Interface Controller, 18
awakeWithContext method
    changing page displayed, 41–43
    initializing Interface Controller, 13, 20–22
    passing/retrieving data, 32–33

B

Background action button
    function of, 163
    for notifications, 150
Background fetch, implementing, 188–192
Background image
    Button control, 56–59
    setting Interface Controller, 65–67
    on Static Interface Controller, 160–161
becomeCurrentPage method, for changing display
        page, 43
body key, 174
Button control
    adding to Interface Controller, 46–47, 83, 86–87
    attributed strings and, 51
    changing background image, 56–59
    changing title dynamically, 50
    creating outlet for, 49–50
    creating/naming action for, 47–49, 114, 126
    custom fonts and, 52–55
    duplicating, 88
    features of, 46
    hierarchical navigation and, 23–24
    localization and, 100–101
    moving into Group control, 88–90
    in navigating using code, 36–37
    page-based navigation and, 27
Buttons project, 46–47

C

Cancel button
    customizing title of, 34–35
    page-based navigation and, 27–28
Chevron (<)
    customizing title of, 34–35
    in hierarchical navigation, 26
Color change for sash/title, 177
Controls (views)
    Button. See Button control
    Date, 112–113
    Group, 86–91
    Image. See Image control
    Label. See Label control
    Map, 123–125
    Menu, 91–92
    Menu Item, 91, 93–94, 97–98
    Slider, 62–65
    Switch, 59–61
    Table. See Table control
CoreLocation.framework, for location data, 115–116
currentDateToString method, in background
        fetch, 189, 191

Custom fonts
    getting names of, 55–56
    using, 52–55
Customization
    chevron/cancel button, 34–35
    Date control, 112–113
    font, 52–55
    glance, 182–185

D

Data
    passing between controllers, 28–33
    retrieving, 138–139
    saving in shared app group, 135–138
dataToPhone dictionary, passing data and, 127
dataToWatch dictionary
    accessing web services, 129–130
    for current location data, 119–120
Date control
    customizing, 112–113
    in different languages, 113
dateStringToDate: method of accepting
        information, 193–194
Device-specific images, 56–57
Dictation, inputs via, 84–85
Dictionary
    accessing web services, 127–130
    location data via, 115, 119–120
didDeactivate method
    changing page displayed, 41–42
    initializing Interface Controller, 13, 20–22
    passing data to controllers, 32
didReceiveLocalNotification:
        withCompletion: method, for long-look
        interface, 172
didReceiveRemoteNotification:
        withCompletion: method, for long-look
        interface, 172
Digital Crown, 2
Dismiss button, for Static Interface Controller, 154,
        156, 157
Displaying information
    Image control for. See Image control
    Label control for, 65
    Table control for. See Table control
DisplayingGlances project, 180–194
downloadImage: method, in sharing files,
        144–145
Dynamic Interface Controller
    changing sash/title color for, 177
    for long-look interface, 154, 168–173
    setting/displaying icons, 159–160

showing new notifications, 176
simulating delays in displaying, 178

E

Edit Scheme... menu item, 175
Emoji inputs, 85–86

F

Files, selecting/creating in localization, 103–104
First Button item
  on Apple Watch notification, 156
  multiple action buttons and, 161–162
First Interface Controller
  Button control added to, 23–24, 27
  passing data from, 28–33
  returning to, 26
  segue connecting, 25, 27
Fonts
  customizing, 52–55
  getting names of, 55–56
ForceTouch project, 91–97
Force Touch
  adding images to project, 95
  adding Label control with, 96
  adding Menu control with, 91–92
  definition of, 2
  displaying context menu, 94, 97
  Image control added with, 95
  setting Menu item attributes with, 93–94
Foreground action button
  function of, 163
  for notifications, 150

G

Gathering information
  dictation for, 84–85
  emojis for, 85–86
  text inputs for, 82–84
GetCurrentLocation class, 117–120
GetLocation project, 114–123
getLocationWithCompletion: method, for
    location data, 119–120
GlanceController class, 182
Glance Interface Controller
  Attributes Inspector window of, 182–183
  displaying information in, 192–194
  implementing glances, 180–182
Glances
  customizing, 182–185
  implementing, 180–182
  modifying for usefulness, 187–192

overview of, 6, 179
testing, 186
updating, 192–194
Gmail notifications, 150–152
Group control
  adding/modifying Button for, 86–87
  centralizing, 90
  duplicating Button for, 88
  implementing, 90–91
  moving Buttons into, 88–89

H

handleActionWithIdentifier:
    forLocalNotification: method, 163–166
handleActionWithIdentifier:
    forRemoteNotification: method, 163–166
HelloAppleWatch project, 6–14
Hierarchical navigation
  customizing chevron in, 34–35
  displaying data passed via, 33
  between Interface Controllers, 22, 23–26
Horizontal attribute, for Label control, 73

I

Icons, for Apple Watch apps, 159–160
Identifier attribute
  of Interface Controller, 25, 27, 36–39
  of Table Row Controller, 75
Identity Inspector window
  Class attribute in, 12, 30, 169
  of Interface Controller, 18
Image control
  adding to Interface Controller, 67, 145–146
  adding to Table control, 78
  connecting outlet to, 79–80
  creating outlet for, 146
  for long-look interface, 168–169
  performing animations via, 69–71
  programmatically setting, 68–69
  setting attributes for, 79
  setting background for, 65–67
  setting/testing, 68
  uses of, 65
Images
  adding to WatchKit app, 169
  animation, 69–71
  changing background, 56–59, 65–67
  project, 65–71
  setting background, 160–161
  Table control displaying, 78–81
Impact font, 52–55

Include Glance Scene option, 180
Include Notification Scene option, in short-look interface, 153
Info.plist file, adding key to, 120
Information inputs
    dictation, 84–85
    emojis, 85–86
    text inputs for, 82–84
Initialization methods for Interface Controller, 13, 19–22
Interactive notifications, 150–151
InterfaceController class
    content of, 12–13
    selecting, 11–12
Interface Controller(s)
    action button launching, 166
    of Apple Watch app, 11–12
    Attributes Inspector window, 18
    Button control added to, 46–47, 83, 86–87
    changing background of, 65–67
    changing page displayed, 40–43
    connected to Swift class, 18–19
    Date control added to, 112–113
    deactivating, 22
    displaying series of, 37–38
    Glance Interface Controller with, 180–181
    Group control added to, 88–90
    hierarchical navigation, 23–26
    Image control added to, 67–69, 145–146
    initialization methods for, 19–20
    Label control added to, 13, 60, 63, 83, 96
    loading, 20–21
    Map control added to, 124
    Menu control added to, 91–92
    navigating using code, 35–38
    navigation between, 22–23
    page-based navigation, 27–28
    passing data between, 28–33
    Slider control added to, 62–65
    Switch control added to, 59
    Table control added to, 72
iOS app
    adding WatchKit app and, 9–11
    bundle, 4
    communicating with, 5–6
    consuming web services on, 126–130
    getting user location, 115–120, 122
    interfacing with. See Localization
    performing background fetch in, 188–192
    shared app groups and. See Shared app group
    sharing files with watch app, 143–148

iOS notifications, 149–152. See also Notifications
iPhone
    adding target to app, 8–11
    Apple Watch interaction with, 4–5
    creating app for, 6–8
iPhone Simulator
    Apple Watch app on, 142
    changing language on, 105
    displaying downloaded image, 147–148
    resetting to English, 112
    selecting country on, 137–138
    testing app on, 14–15
    unlocking, 22

L
Label control
    adding to Interface Controller, 13, 60, 63, 83, 96
    adding to Table control, 72
    connecting outlet to, 75
    creating outlet for, 30, 114, 126, 164
    features of, 65
    in hierarchical navigation, 25–26
    Lines attribute of, 156–157
    localizing, 102–106
    for long-look interface, 168–169
    naming outlet for, 31
    in navigating using code, 36
    setting attributes for, 73
    for Static Interface Controller, 154
    typing text into, 14
Languages
    Date control and, 112–113
    localization and, 102–106, 109–111
Layouts project, 86–91
Lifecycle of Interface Controller, 19–22
LifeCycle project, 17–19
Lines attribute, setting, 156–157
Local notifications, 149
Localization
    adding string file, 107
    changing language and, 105
    displaying title in, 106
    file selection/addition for, 103–104
    language selection for, 102, 109
    for multiple languages, 99–101
    naming string file and, 108
    project, 100–113
    of string files, 110–112
    string literals used in, 104
Location data
    adding Button/Label controls for, 114

adding new key for, 120
adding Swift file for, 117–118
displaying maps with, 123–125
displaying on Apple Watch, 123
displaying on Label control, 121–122
implementing code for, 118–119, 121
obtaining permission to access, 122
openParentApplication: method in, 115
preparing/adding new framework, 115–116
Long-look interface for notifications
features of, 167
implementing, 168–173
Lower group selections, in customizing glances, 184–185

M

Map control, for location data, 123–125
Menu control, 91–92
Menu Item controls
adding programmatically, 97–98
displaying image, 91, 93, 97
setting attributes for, 93–94
Minus (–) button on Slider control, 62, 64–65
Mode attribute, of Image control, 70

N

NavigateUsingCode project, 36–43
Navigation, of Interface Controller
hierarchical, 23–26
overview of, 22–23
page-based, 27–28
using code, 35–38
NotificationController class, 169–172
Notification Simulation File, 173
Notifications
action buttons for, 163–167
on Apple Watch, 152–153
customizing, 156–157
definition of, 149
long-look interface for, 167–172
other payloads for simulating, 173–176
overview of, 6
overview of iOS, 150–152
project, 153–178
setting background image for, 160–161
short-look interface for, 153–156
types of, 149–150
NSLocationAlways-UsageDescription key, 120–122
NSURLConnection class, downloading images and, 144–145
NSURLSession class, connecting to web service, 129–130

NSUserDefaults setting
in background fetch, 187, 189–191
saving data and, 135–137, 193

O

openParentApplication: method, passing data to iOS app, 115, 120, 127–129
Options button, for notifications, 151–152

P

Page-based navigation
changing page displayed and, 40–43
customizing Cancel button in, 34–35
displaying data passed via, 33–34
displaying series of pages and, 38–40
between Interface Controllers, 22–23, 27–28
parseJSONData: method
connecting to web service, 129–130
extracting data, 189–190
Picker view, saving data and, 135–137
Plus (+) button on Slider control, 62, 64–65
presentControllerWithName:context: method
displaying series of pages, 38–40
in page-based navigation, 37–38
presentTextInputControllerWithSuggestions: method
for emojis, 85–86
for text inputs, 82–84
Push notifications, 149
pushControllerWithName:context: method, in hierarchical navigation, 37–38
PushNotificationPayload.apns file, 154–156, 161–163
PushNotificationPayload-delayed.apns file, 173–176

R

Remote notifications
definition of, 149
with multiple action buttons, 161–163
Reply button, for notifications, 150–151
replyDataFromPhone dictionary, 127–128
Resolutions, of Apple Watch sizes, 1–2
Root.plist file, 141–142

S

Sash color, changing, 177
Second Interface Controller
Cancel button on, 27–28
Label control added to, 25
passing data to, 28–33
Segue, in hierarchical navigation, 24–25, 32–33
Selectable attribute, of Row controller, 75, 81

setImageNamed: method, 68–69
setMinimumBackgroundFetchInterval method, 190–191
Shared app group
    adding to WatchKit Extension, 187–188
    creating/adding to iOS project, 187
    development team/app group for, 133
    enrolling in Apple Developer Program, 131–132
    entering Apple ID/password, 132
    for extension target, 134–135
    naming new container for, 133–134
    retrieving data from, 138–139
    saving data in, 135–138
    sharing files and, 143–148
    turning on Capabilities feature, 131
    viewing newly created app group, 134
Short-look interface for notifications
    implementing, 153–156
    with multiple action buttons, 161–163
Single View Application, creating, 6–7
Slider control
    adding/testing, 62
    creating outlet for, 63
    setting attributes for, 63–64
    Steps attribute and, 64–65
Sliders project, 62–65
Specifications, Apple Watch, 1–2
Static Interface Controller
    changing sash/title color for, 177
    customizing notifications on, 156–157
    displaying action buttons, 161–163
    modifying display name on, 158
    reverting back to, 178
    setting background image for, 160–161
    setting/displaying icons, 159–160
    for short-look interface, 154
Steps attribute, for Slider control, 64–65
Stock prices
    background fetch of, 188–190
    retrieving, 193
Storyboard Editor, examining, 11–12
Storyboard file
    adding Interface Controllers to, 23, 154
    background image in, 59
    drag/drop Button onto, 46
    editing, 18
    selecting, 17
String files
    adding, 107
    language selection for, 109
    localization of, 110–112
    naming, 108

Swift class
    adding to project, 73
    assigning Table control to, 74
    for current location data, 117–118
Switch control
    adding to Interface Controller, 59
    changing title of, 59–60
    creating outlet for, 60
    testing, 61
Switches project, 59–62

T
Table control
    adding to Interface Controller, 71–72
    adding/assigning to Swift class, 73–74
    connecting image outlet in, 79–80
    creating outlet for, 76
    displaying images in rows, 81
    displaying list of items, 77
    features of, 71
    Image control added to, 78
    Image control attributes and, 79
    Label control added to, 72
    selecting items via, 81–82
    setting Table Row Controller Identifier, 75
Table Row Controller
    adding Image control to, 78
    Identifier attribute for, 75
    selecting, 74
table:didSelectRowAtIndex: method, 81–82
Tables project, 71–82
Taptic Engine, 2
TextInputs project, 83–85
Text inputs, 82–85
timeIntervalSinceDate: method, of retrieving information, 193–194
Title color, changing, 177

U
UI (user interface) controls
    Button. See Button control
    Date, 112–113
    Group, 86–91
    Image. See Image control
    Label, 65
    obtaining inputs and, 82–86
    overview of, 45
    Slider, 62–65
    Switch, 59–61
    Table. See Table control
UI (user interface) localizations, 102–106

UINavigation project, 23–34
Upper group selections, in customized glances, 183
User interaction response controls
    Button. *See* Button control
    overview of, 45
    Slider, 62–65
    Switch, 59–61
UserInfo argument
    in accessing web services, 128, 130
    passing data to iOS app, 118, 120

V

Vertical attribute, for Label control, 73
View Controller, saving data and, 135–137
Views. *See* Controls (views)

W

WatchKit app
    adding images to, 169
    adding to iPhone app, 8–11
    adding/naming font file in, 52–54
    deploying, 4
    function of, 3–4
    interaction with WatchKit Extension, 3–4
    lifecycle of, 12–13
    modifying name of, 158
    overview of, 6
    Settings app for, 140–143
WatchKit Extension
    adding shared app group to, 187–188
    adding to iPhone app, 10–11
    adding/naming font file in, 52–53

function of, 3–4
    interaction with WatchKit app, 3–4
WatchKit framework
    types of applications, 6
    understanding, 3–6
WatchKit Settings Bundle
    adding items to, 142
    naming/viewing file in, 141
    selecting, 140
Weather information access, 126–130, 138–139
Web service access, 126–130
WebServices project, 126–148
willActivate method
    changing page displayed, 41–42
    initializing Interface Controller, 13, 20–22
    passing data to controllers, 32
    updating glances, 182
WKInterfaceController class
    GlanceController class extending, 182
    naming subclass of, 29
    subclassing, 12–13

X

Xcode
    for Apple Watch apps, 2
    background fetch and, 191, 192
    creating iPhone app in, 6–8
    Output Window in, 21–22
    in testing app, 14

Y

Yahoo web service connection, 188–190